ESSE

YEAR
ROUND
WALKS

Spring, Summer, Autumn & Winter

Len Banister

COUNTRYSIDE BOOKS
NEWBURY BERKSHIRE

First published 2012
© Len Banister 2012

COUNTRYSIDE BOOKS
3 Catherine Road
Newbury, Berkshire

To view our complete range of books,
please visit us at
www.countrysidebooks.co.uk

ISBN 978 1 84674 251 4

Designed by Peter Davies, Nautilus Design
Produced through MRM Associates Ltd., Reading
Printed by Information Press, Oxford

Contents

Contents

Autumn

Winter

Introduction

You will be hard pressed these days to escape the message that regular walking is the healthiest of activities. In this book I hope to encourage you to walk all the year round and, to do this, I have made a selection of routes for each of the four seasons.

Essex is always a surprise to the novice walker who may think of it as a county offering few opportunities for variety or interest. This is my fourth book of walks in Essex, eighty walks in all, and I have had little difficulty in coming up with an exciting selection of brand new outings. We visit a fort on the coast at Tilbury, climb the hills of Langdon, amble through the countryside that Constable painted, wonder at the efforts to restore an 18th-century house all but destroyed by fire – and, all the time, we have the continually changing background of nature.

It is this natural rhythm of nature through the seasons that makes walking all the year round such a wonderful and rewarding activity and renders my seasonal selections so arbitrary because, of course, these walks will be delightful at any time.

What I have tried to do is to recommend walks when either the conditions are more suitable or when the seasonal variation is at its most interesting. As a rule of thumb I have selected winter walks that are most likely to be dry underfoot; summer walks that are likely to be shady; autumn outings when leafless trees are likely to reveal the best views; and spring, when I believe that walking is always at its very best, for the remainder.

Each walk is circular and is fully described so that you will safely complete the route. A simple map accompanies each excursion – in addition, I recommend that you also take the relevant Ordnance Survey Explorer sheet with you so that you can identify the surrounding countryside and plan your own diversions.

Whilst I always try to provide additional information about the area you will visit, I have made a particular feature of something to look out for on each trip. To make your day complete I also recommend where you can find a café or pub for refreshment.

It is many years ago that I resolved to go on a good walk at least once a week, whatever the weather. I sincerely hope that this book will go some way to persuading you to take a similar decision.

Len Banister

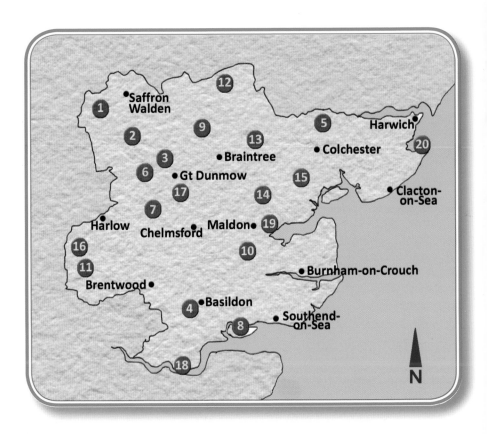

PUBLISHER'S NOTE

We hope that you obtain considerable enjoyment from this book; great care has been taken in its preparation. Although at the time of publication all routes followed public rights of way or permitted paths, diversion orders can be made and permissions withdrawn.

We cannot, of course, be held responsible for such diversion orders and any inaccuracies in the text which result from these or any other changes to the routes nor any damage which might result from walkers trespassing on private property. We are anxious, though, that all details covering the walks are kept up to date and would therefore welcome information from readers which would be relevant to future editions.

The simple sketch maps that accompany the walks in the book are based on notes made by the author whilst checking out the routes on the ground. For the benefit of a proper map, however, we do recommend that you purchase the relevant Ordnance Survey sheet covering your walk. The Ordnance Survey maps are widely available, especially through booksellers and local newsagents.

1 *Elmdon*

The Hamlet church and Church House.

This is a spring walk that shows Essex at its best. Gentle rolling countryside, almost manicured in places, has that green freshness which brings with it the promise of more delights later in the year. Just as the trees are coming into bud so, underneath, bluebells are quickly displaying their wares before the sunshine is shut off by the canopy to come – these carpets of colour will add that extra dressing to what will be a treat at any time of the year. This is a great walk for variety. We see lots of views across the neighbouring countryside and descend into attractive valleys with imposing houses and estates.

Distance 5½ miles.

Terrain Although this is the highest area of Essex, any hills are so slight that you are unlikely to get out of breath. There are some very good tracks but, as usual at this time of the year, be prepared for some muddy field edges after rain.

Map Explorer 194 Hertford & Bishop's Stortford.

Starting point The Elmdon Dial pub where the landlord is happy for walkers to use the car park (GR TL461397).

How to get there Elmdon is signed northwards off the B1039, which runs between Royston and Wendens Ambo. The pub car park is nearly opposite the church.

Refreshments The Elmdon Dial is almost the definition of a walker-friendly pub. Named after the famous window in the church opposite, it reopened, completely and tastefully refurbished, in 2006 and provides a very comfortable climax to the day's outing. The bar menu ranges from baguettes or ciabatta to some straightforward but superbly-cooked traditional meals. There is also a restaurant. The pub is closed on Mondays. Food is not available in the bar on Sundays but the restaurant is open for Sunday lunch. ☎ 01763 837386.

The Walk

1 Leave the pub car park and turn left along the road, looking carefully for a stile on the left. Once over, follow a hedge to cross two more stiles before joining a left field edge. Cross a field boundary before a thatched house and turn right alongside a ditch; soon leave the field edge to aim for a gap in the hedge to the left ahead. Pass between lakes and turn right and follow the field edge to a waymarker and go through **King's Grove** into an adjoining field.

2 Turn left then, at the boundary, right, ignoring a path to the left, then going right alongside **Park Wood**. Keep forward through a barrier to cross **Parkhouse Lane** and join a semi-surfaced byway, which you leave by turning left at the next waymarker to follow a clear cross-field path. (You are now, briefly, on the **Icknield Way**; a route claimed to be the oldest in Britain, running from Ivinghoe Beacon in Buckinghamshire to Knettishall Heath in Norfolk.) Join a

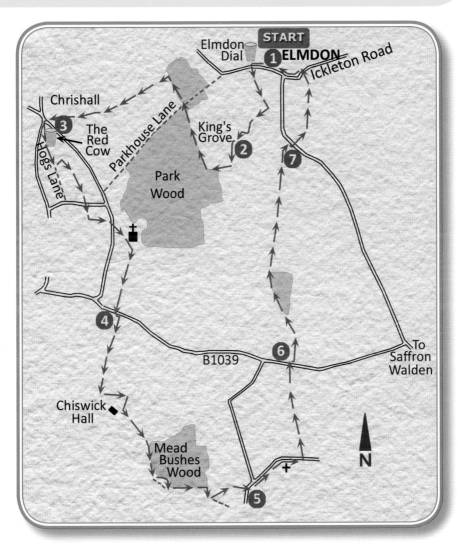

fence on the left to reach a stile then continue with the hedge on the right. Pass through a metal kissing-gate to reach a road in the village of **Chrishall**.

3 Cross to the left of the war memorial and turn left on **Hog's Lane** in front of the **Red Cow** pub (you are now on the **Harcamlow Path**). After the last of the houses go left on a field edge and follow this along backs of gardens to finally reach a lane. Cross and join a grassy track to the right of a hedge then follow a waymarker onto a fenced path to a lane. Cross slightly left to a bridge. After another bridge, follow a fence up to keep forward across the churchyard

Chiswick Hall, passed at point 4 of the walk.

and leave by a gate. Now keep ahead, downhill, on a broad cross-field path to a footbridge and road.

4 Go diagonally left to join a drive uphill. Near the top, go left to walk along a wooden fenced hedge on a path that goes around the 17th-century **Chiswick Hall** and ends at a hedge that juts out. Go left downhill here to cross a bridge and reach the boundary of **Mead Bushes Wood**. Go right uphill with the boundary and follow it round until you reach a waymarker where you turn right to walk with the hedge to your left. Cross a bridge and turn left along the field edge to a road.

5 Go left across a bridge and fork right at the junction.

On the left is the Hamlet church. In 1859 the local Squire Parson took pity on the villagers of Duddenhoe End who had to walk all the way to Elmdon to pray so he converted the 17th-century tithe barn into a church. Whilst a thatched church is unusual, the fact that the altar is set on the long, eastern, side of the building is more so. The church is always open and is well worth a visit to see its simple brushed pine pews with attached candlesticks.

After passing the cemetery, look for a fingerpost on the left which takes you downhill. Halfway down, follow the path into the trees and continue to the road.

6 Cross diagonally right to a bridge and walk up the other side of the valley, with **Mill House** to the left. Follow the beech hedge until it turns very sharply left – at this point, carry straight on at a fingerpost. At the next field boundary, go right over a bridge, through a strip of woodland, and over a stile to join a wide, fenced path. Ignore all side paths for ½ mile (notice the way that horses have chewed away at the expensive fencing). Continue along the right edge of a sports field to a road.

7 Go diagonally right to join a path between houses. Swing right into another field then left down the field edge and on to a gate over to the right of farm buildings. Go through another gate to reach **Ickleton Road** at Elmdon. Cross diagonally left to enter the churchyard (the window with the Elmdon Dial is facing you) and rejoin the road to go right to the pub.

What to look out for –

On your return to Elmdon you are guided through the churchyard. The window of St Nicholas' church, which faces you, bears a piece of 17th-century stained glass known as the **Elmdon Dial**. The glass, which was originally made for another church, was produced at a time of Puritan rule when little church decoration was manufactured and artists restricted themselves to images that could not be considered papist. The design, which includes an hour-glass, a sun dial and a fly (which represents disease), was supposed to remind the congregation about the fleeting nature of life and the

Latin inscriptions translate as *Such is life!* and *No day without a line*. If he is not too busy, the landlord of the pub named after the dial can sometimes be persuaded to give more historic details of this important window.

↻② *Widddington*

The path alongside the juvenile Cam.

Widdington is a quiet village set in one of the most beautiful areas of Essex. As a spring walk this provides a backdrop opportunity to observe the awakening of plant life after the rigour of winter. Interspersed on the route, alongside the juvenile River Cam and the glorious wooded areas, are some splendid houses and a couple of magnificent churches. When you return in the summer, as you surely will, you will be amazed at the changed aspect – not least by the rich banks of blackberries ready for harvest.

Distance 5 miles.

Terrain Although the surrounding countryside is beautifully undulating, the actual walk is quite flat. Some of the shaded woodland paths take time to dry out after rain but you can normally avoid mud.

Map OS Explorer 195 Braintree & Saffron Walden.

Starting point Alongside the small triangular green near the church in the centre of the village (GR TL538318).

How to get there Leave the M11 at junction 8 or 9 to join the B1383. Widdington is signposted south of Newport.

Refreshments The Fleur De Lys pub is passed at the start of the walk. It has an excellently varied menu and is housed in a low-timbered, attractive building, where children and dogs are welcomed. ☎ 01799 543280.

The Walk

❶ Walk along **South Green** with the village pump to the left and continue forward on **High Street**, soon passing the **Fleur de Lys** pub on the left. Continue into **Wood End**, passing a pond on the left and eventually being confronted by the imposing **Widdington House**.

❷ Go left alongside the house. The track passes a house and then becomes an enclosed lane. Stay with the track to enter **Prior's Wood**, taking an early fork left and quickly another to the right. You will now follow a relatively straight track through the wood to reach a gate. Go straight across the middle of the field beyond to pass through a narrow band of trees to a cross-track.

❸ Turn left with a stream to your right. (This 'stream' is actually the **River Cam** or **Granta**, which will eventually flow under the Bridge of Sighs in Cambridge and feed the Great Ouse, south of Ely.) Keep forward past a bridge on the right. Eventually the track swings away from the river and starts to climb between trees. Reach **Cornells Lane**.

❹ Go left and immediately right. (The banks of this lane are sprinkled with periwinkle and violets in springtime.) Keep to the lane as it swings right in front of the drive to **Swayne's Hall**. Soon you pass **Mole Hall** on the right.

Spring

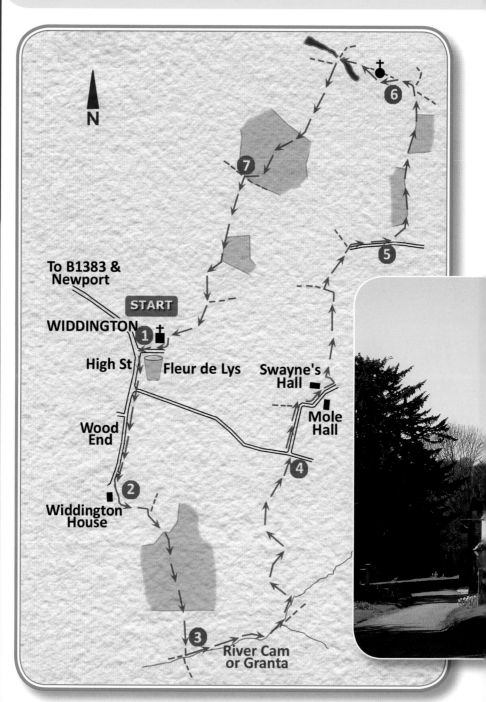

N

To B1383 &
Newport

START

WIDDINGTON

High St

Fleur de Lys

Wood
End

Widdington
House

Swayne's
Hall

Mole
Hall

River Cam
or Granta

1
2
3
4
5
6
7

Continue past some dilapidated stables to turn left in front of a hedged path. Just around the corner, at a waymarker, continue right along the left edge of a field. In the following field go left and follow the field edge around to the right. Soon the path feeds into a track, then a lane; you go straight past the first of several thatched cottages – this one has a flagpole. Reach a concrete fingerpost on the left.

5 Go diagonally left across a field to cross a bridge. Turn left. The path soon leaves the field to go inside the edge of **Spinney Wood**. Follow this delightful path, eventually crossing an earth bridge into a meadow. Go ahead, passing to the right of the hedge corner opposite to reach a junction of drives.

6 Go left past a small car park into the churchyard of **Debden church**. Walk to the left of the church to pick up a narrow path between gravestones and leave by an old metal gate. Keep left along a fenced path to reach an intriguing farm

Spring

Debden church.

building on the right at a T-junction. Go left over a bridge and keep forward on a wide track across the middle of a field, ignoring a turning to the right, and continue into **Cabbage Wood**.

7 Emerge from the wood with a derelict cottage to the right and barn to the left. Cross the main track to go straight across the field to the right of **Park Wood** ahead. At the end of the wood, go across a footbridge and head diagonally slightly right across the next field. At the far side, turn right to continue along the field edge. Go left at the corner then right into the churchyard of **Widdington church**. Leave by the main gate and go right to your car.

What to look out for –

Two grand houses almost opposite each other are passed during stage 4:

Mole Hall is a moated manor house that is mentioned in the Domesday Book and dates from 1287. Its grounds have housed a wildlife park and tropical house for many years. The park, which opens in late April until September, also has rare breed farm animals and wetlands that attract birdlife. There is a café on the site. ☎ 01799 540400.

Swayne's Hall clearly displays the date of its construction, 1689, on the house front. If you look more closely, you can see, on the right-hand side between the first floor windows, nine original pargeted panels illustrating flowers, a couple of lions and fleur-de-lys.

⟳(3) *Stebbing*

Daffodils cover the mound of the Norman castle in springtime.

The High Street area of Stebbing is itself worth a wander before or after this walk. The mix of Tudor and Georgian houses has been lovingly restored to provide the kind of scene that typifies the image of an English village.

We leave the High Street via the church using quiet lanes and byways to reach the hamlet of Bardfield Saling. Our return emphasises extensive views across the neighbouring countryside before visiting the mound and moat of a Norman castle. This is a walk for sunny spring days when the tracks are dry; the trees are in bud although still bare enough to reveal the vestiges of last year's nests; and the hawthorn is in bloom. If you go in late March, you will have the bonus of violets and daffodils in the verges and a complete carpet of primroses in the churchyard at Bardfield Saling.

Spring

The Facts

Distance 6½ miles.

Terrain This is an easy, flat walk. Most of the route is on quiet lanes or byways. The latter are indicated on your OS map by chains of green crosses; they are also known as BOATS: Byways Open to All Traffic. You may theoretically meet motorcycles or four-wheel drive vehicles but for our route this is unlikely. One section at the start of stage 2 can be rutted but this shouldn't worry you in the spring.

Map OS Explorer 195 Braintree & Saffron Walden.

Starting point Roadside parking along the High Street, near the White Hart pub (GR TL661243).

How to get there Turn off to Great Dunmow from the A120 to pick up the B1256; Stebbing is signposted off to the north.

Refreshments The White Hart is a comfortable pub with an unpretentious menu. It also brews its own beer, which joins a selection of other real ales. It is closed from 3 pm to 5 pm during the week but open all day at weekends. ☎ 01371 856383.

The Walk

1 Walk down the **High Street** towards the church. Climb the steps into the churchyard and continue, to the right of the church, to exit through a gate to a road where you go left. After passing houses, go along the road for a further field-width then go left, up a bank, to proceed along a left-hand field edge. Descend to a dip, cross a field boundary and continue in the next field until you reach a junction with a waymarker; now turn right and go straight across the field to a gap in the hedge. Cross a track and go forward in the next field, gradually veering to the right to a gap roughly halfway along the hedge in front. Once through, go slightly right across the field to another gap and pass alongside the wall of **Lucas Farm House**, across a drive and green, to a lane. Go left.

2 When you come to the white gates of **Gatehouse Farm** on the right, go in and keep to the main track, ignoring a bridge on the left. Reach a concrete standing and keep forward with long sheds over to the left. Arriving at a T-junction with **Badcocks Farm** to the right, turn left alongside a small pond. Reach a pair of concrete fingerposts just before houses.

3 Turn right. At the next junction go left on a track (**Rogue's Green**), which is so closely hedged that you are almost walking through a tunnel. The trees gradually thin out, reconnecting you with the landscape. Soon after **Gentleman's Farm** you arrive at a road.

4 Turn left. Over to your left you can usually see commercially raised deer. Ahead is the **church of St Peter and St Paul** of **Bardfield Saling** with its unusual round tower. Opposite is the fine old house of **Arundels** with its highly active dovecot and offer of local honey for sale. You will no doubt wish to examine the church but our path goes left before it by a post box. Walk along the right edge of a field and keep to it until you cross a bridge to a lane.

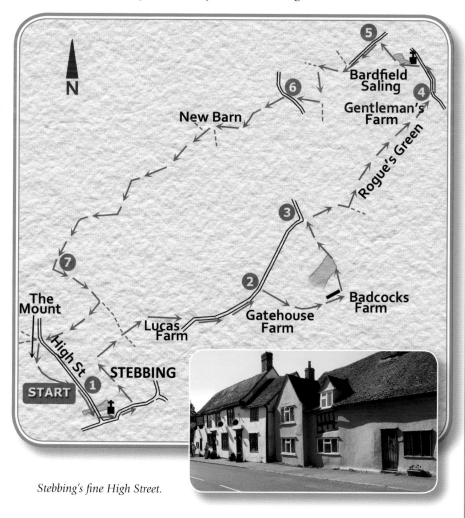

Stebbing's fine High Street.

Spring

5 Go left. Keep forward along a drive labelled as a 'dead end' and ignore a track to the right. At the next junction fork left and go on to swing right and finally reach a lane.

6 Turn right; after about 60 yards go left along a signed byway. When you reach the large barn of **New Barn Farm** with several cross-tracks, keep forward, passing white barriers, to join a track with a ditch and hedge on each side. At the next junction, cross a stream and swing right to eventually reach buildings and a lane.

7 Turn left on the lane, which soon becomes another tree-lined track. At a junction alongside a field boundary go right, slightly down a slope, alongside a reassuring waymarker that takes you along the right edge of a field. Follow this hedge until just before the houses when, at a multiple waymarker, you switch sides but keep forward, now on a narrow path, behind houses to reach an estate road. Go right and cross the main road to join the drive of **Stebbing Park** and immediately go left to take a gated path alongside a fence on the right. This takes you alongside **The Mount** – the mound of a Norman castle with its moat. (Beware of holes made by very determined rabbits.) Cross a bridge and keep forward to enter a playing field; now go diagonally left towards a converted chapel and exit to the right of its wall. In the lane turn left to reach the High Street by the **White Hart**.

What to look out for –

Although round-towered churches are common in Norfolk, where there are 126, and in Suffolk, where there are 42, there are only 6 in Essex. **The church of St Peter and St Paul** is probably the last medieval example built in Britain – its construction was thought to have been delayed by the Black Death. It is still standing upright despite being dedicated by the Bishop of Pisa in the early 14th century.

4 The Langdon Hills

Banks of wildflowers fill the wooded areas of the route.

This is a walk for a fine day in April when banks of field mouse-ear, bluebells and anemones in the thickly wooded areas will vie for your attention with views across the Thames Estuary to Kent. It is also a walk on which to take the visitor who is convinced that Essex is a flat county – here are inclines and descents that will make you hot and out of breath on a summer's day.

Much of the walk is through Langdon Hills Country Park, which is split into two sections known as Westley Heights and One Tree Hill. Footpaths and horse/cycle rides pass through attractive farmland between the various sections, providing extensive areas of accessible countryside where, even on the busiest Sunday afternoon, visitors may find a quiet corner to relax and enjoy the peaceful scenery.

21

Spring

The Facts

Distance 5¼ miles.

Terrain This is one of the more rigorous walks in the book. There are a couple of quite steep climbs, which are rewarded with excellent views. Numerous springs result in small streams that cross the path in places, so be prepared for muddy patches at times.

Map OS Explorer 175 Southend-on-Sea & Basildon.

Starting point The Langdon Hills Country Park free car park at GR TQ697859. Check the times of gate closure, which vary.

How to get there The country park is south-west of Basildon. Take a turning off the B1007 alongside the Harvester pub onto Dry Street. Now look for a lane signposted to the Memorial Church and Langdon Hills. Go past one car park, right at the start of this lane, then another which has a visitor centre and lavatories, to reach a third at the bottom of the hill on the right.

Refreshments A short diversion during stage 5 will take you to the Harvester pub on the B1007 that you passed on your way to the start; open daily from 11 am to 11 pm. ☎ 01268 544714.

The Walk

❶ Walk back to the road and cross it diagonally right to go through a barrier and join a wide path. Continue, passing a dog bin on the left, to later pass one path and immediately go left at another alongside a gate. Take the middle of three paths on offer; ignore one turning right but, at the next, turn right on a narrower path towards a fence – before reaching this, turn left on a cross-track. Fork right to walk along the edge of a stream (notice the temple-like building in the trees to your right). Go right over a footbridge to emerge on the right edge of a field. Keep forward past a barrier on a semi-surfaced path and swing left with it uphill. Arrive at a T-junction.

❷ Go right. All the time you are climbing gently and views are opening up to the right. The track peters out at the top of the hill but you continue swinging around to the right across a meadow, with unusual buildings to the left. On reaching the lower corner, go through a gap in the hedge and forward to a lane.

Bluebells, anemones and field mouse-ear border the paths.

3 Turn left. Continue to the right of the entrance to **Hawkesbury Manor** at a fingerpost. Emerge on a field edge and go left. Keep the hedge to the left in the first two fields, and to the right in the third. Before the next field, avoid a farm track and continue with the hedge and **Dry Street Farm** to the right. Cross a stile and walk to the right of the unprepossessing **Memorial Church** ahead. Go through a metal kissing-gate and turn right on a lane to a road.

4 Cross diagonally left through a barrier into **Willow Park Nature Reserve**. Keep forward (later paths to the left take you to a series of ponds, which you may wish to explore) for about ½ mile. Eventually the track reaches its peak, goes slightly downhill and swings left. Keep following the track, ignoring a barrier and then a turning to the right. Pass a track to the left to **Kingston Ridge Scout campsite**. (Later you can go left through a barrier to inspect a lake on the left and continue to rejoin the main path.) Leave the nature reserve and pass a car park on the right.

Spring

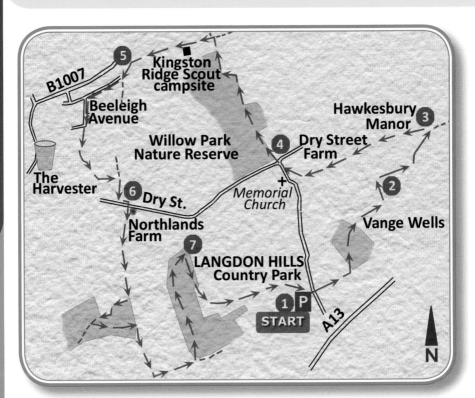

5 Keep forward as the track becomes a drive between houses. Go left on **Beeleigh Avenue**. Where this swings to the left, fork right along a path to a gate then keep forward along a valley to reach a display map with a roof. (*To visit the pub, go right through a car park, passing a picnic area on the left, to leave the boundary of the country park and walk up a slope – you are now in the pub's car park.*) With your back to the display map, take the right-hand path with a bench to the right. Go downhill to a T-junction and turn left, passing a line of three character seats. Where the surfaced path turns sharply left, go right through a gate along a narrow hedged path to reach a drive, then a road (**Dry Street**).

6 Go left then right at the end of buildings along a concrete farm drive (the gate may be locked but you can go beside it) with a lake to the left. Keep forward all the way through **Northlands Farm** and continue on a track down the right edge of a field. At the bottom, go right through a metal kissing-gate. Follow the route around the edge of the fields through a series of gates. After the final gate in the series, exit by a metal kissing-gate in the left-hand corner of the last field. Reach a track and go left, and go left again at the next junction. Swing right at post 11, now with arable land to the left. The path swings left. Just before it begins to go steeply uphill at a junction (post 12), go left at a gate. Keep left at an early fork and later ignore a fork to the right. Eventually you come to a T-junction; there is a gate over to the left but you turn right.

7 At a fork (post 14), go left. Ignore a fork to the right. Later the path goes steeply downhill then rises again. Look for a bench overlooking open ground on the right with steps to the left. Descend right, going to the left of a large clump of trees, beyond which you will see the car park.

What to look out for –

During a drought in 1900, a local farmer used some foul-smelling water drawn from a well for his cattle. The animals not only survived but thrived, so entrepreneur and self-styled farmer and appropriately named Edwin Cash, licensee of the Angel in Islington, seized the opportunity to sink another well. In 1919, when he retired as a publican, Farmer Cash started to sell bottles of the water, which bore a signed photograph of him under the trade name of 'Vange Mineral Water'. The business flourished, supported by testimonials in *The Lancet*. Besides selling to local chemists, Cash catered for increasing numbers of visitors wishing to 'take the waters', and eventually, in 1923, he built the domed Classical-temple-like structure over the well. You can see the derelict remains of this enterprise during the first stage of the walk – **Vange Well No 5**. Unfortunately for the business, a sanatorium for the treatment of people with tuberculosis was opened higher up the hill. It is believed that drainage from this contaminated the well water and Farmer Cash's business had to stop trading.

Spring

Spring

The River Stour meanders through delightful watermeadows.

This walk is a sheer delight. Making much use of two major footpaths, the St Edmund Way and the Essex Way, we meander alongside the River Stour on both sides of the Essex/Suffolk border in the most beautiful meadows imaginable. It's no wonder that one of England's most famous painters, John Constable, spent so much time transferring the bucolic scenes of this area onto canvas. You have the option of extending this outing to visit the famous Flatford Mill, which, along with glimpses of Dedham church on the return route, provides further familiar images of the artist's work. The walk purposely explores the town of Dedham, which is crowded with memorable buildings and shops. The popularity of this area means that this walk is best done on a weekday, thus avoiding the crowds.

The Facts

Spring

Distance 4¼ miles (plus 1½ miles if you visit Flatford Mill).

Terrain Most of this walk is along the flood-plain of the river and is very flat with few stiles. Given the situation, it is quite likely that the meadows will be spongy during the spring when water levels are high.

Map OS Explorer 196 Sudbury, Hadleigh & Dedham Vale.

Starting point The small layby with room for three or four cars almost opposite the large Le Talbooth Hotel and Restaurant at GR TM043335 (avoid blocking access to the tunnel under the A12).

How to get there Langham is situated just off the A12 between Colchester and Ipswich. The starting point for the walk is on a road that runs along the west side of the A12 and is at the northern side of the River Stour.

Refreshments There are restaurants, pubs and tearooms in Dedham. The Sun Inn is particularly recommended – and its wooden floors are ideal for walkers in inclement weather. The superb main meals and the bargain bar meals are all served in a low-beamed, homely atmosphere with interesting paintings on the walls. ☎ 01206 323351.

The Walk

❶ Leave the parking area by walking along a tunnel under the A12. Go through a kissing-gate and immediately join the bank of the **River Stour**, which will become a main feature of this walk. Soon the noise of the road is lost as you wander along the glorious meadows, separated by occasional gates. As you approach the main road at **Dedham Bridge**, it is worth diverting to cross a bridge to the right to examine the weir at **Dedham Lock** and its relationship with the **Mill** (now converted into apartments). Reach the main road.

❷ Cross diagonally left to go through a gate and rejoin the river bank. After the first field boundary, keep forward on the path. This takes you away from the river bank to go through a gate with a National Trust sign about 100 yards to the left of the Stour.

❸ Continue on a secluded hedged path to reach a junction. Fork right and then go right on a cross-track to reach a bridge by which you cross the river.

4 (*If you follow the river bank to the left for ¾ mile you will reach* **Flatford Mill**, *once owned by John Constable's father and, along with the nearby* **Willy Lott's Cottage**, *a main feature of many of the artist's paintings.*) To continue the main circuit, go right alongside the river (*continuing westwards beside the river if coming from Flatford Mill*) to the first field boundary. Once through the gate, go diagonally left across the next pasture to join another beautiful hedged path in the right-hand corner. Continue up a rise and ignore turnings to the left to follow a track which forks left at a Business Centre and becomes a drive, which you follow to the corner of **Brook Street**.

5 Go immediately sharp right along a drive; just before the forked entrance to **Dedham Hall**, go left through a gate, alongside a lake to the left. Keep forward to the left-hand corner of a small pasture. Ignore a bridge to the left and follow a stream to a stile. Go left across a ford and arrive at a road with the Mill opposite.

Dedham Hall seen from the route.

6 Cross and go left. At the **High Street** go right (passing the **Sun Inn** and numerous other attractive buildings). Continue past **Princel Lane** and, about 100 yards later, turn right at a footpath sign at the drive to **Westgate Cottage**. This feeds into a farm track. Continue through **Bridges Farm** and follow the track along the right-hand side of the next field, but look for the **Essex Way** sign, which takes you, via a Victorian kissing-gate, through the hedge to continue on the other side. In the next meadow, keep forward, passing a redundant stile, to go through another old gate and veer slightly left to cross a stile.

7 Arrive at a drive with a car park to the right and go left. Just before a junction go right and walk along the right-hand side of a road; this crosses the A12. After the road-bridge, go right at a junction. After passing the **Talbooth** and crossing the Stour you will see the layby on the right.

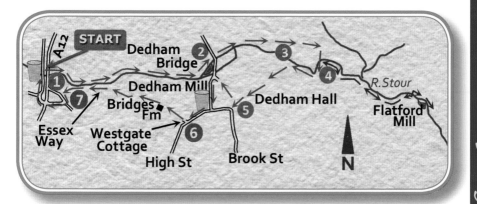

Spring

What to look out for –

Wood has been harvested from the Dedham Vale willows for hundreds of years. The technique involved is known as **pollarding**. This is where wood is cut some six or eight feet or so from the ground, beheading the tree. The new shoots can grow out of reach of the browsing livestock. Traditionally trees would be pollarded on a 5- to 15-year cycle and the resulting timber would be used for fencing and building whilst the foliage would supplement the diet of cattle. At the time of writing, many of the willows had been cut for the first time in over 20 years and they will be bursting with fresh growth in the springtime. The motive for this work was more to do with preserving the views of the valley as seen in Constable's day than with any modern-day commercial consideration.

6 Church End, Great Dunmow

Looking across the lake at Old Dunmow.

Great Dunmow is rapidly expanding. This walk starts by taking you through some of the more interesting parts of the old town, out on a long-abandoned railway track and into the countryside to the delightful hamlet of Little Easton Manor. It is on the return trip that you will appreciate the increasing growth of the town and the continuing efforts on the part of the planners to retain as much as is possible of the attractive countryside. This is a walk for the early summer, featuring, as it does, startling displays of wild flowers, placid lakes replete with wildfowl and the signature big skies of Essex.

Distance 5¼ miles.

Terrain This is an easy walk with no stiles, mainly on the level. (If walking in wintertime here, you should be prepared for mud.) During stage 7 you may discover some variations to the route resulting from house building – these will be well signed and should cause few problems.

Map OS Explorer 195 Braintree & Saffron Walden.

Starting point A spacious free parking area near the church in Church End (GR TL628230).

How to get there Take the A120 from junction 8 of the M11. Turn off, when Great Dunmow is indicated, onto the B1256. Go through the town centre and join the B184 going north. Turn off this onto the B1057 towards Church End then turn off left along Church Street. Continue on a narrow lane, passing to the left of the church, to reach the car park.

Refreshments Very soon after the start of the walk you will pass the Angel and Harp. It is open and serves meals all day, with an emphasis on pizzas, burgers, salads and snacks. ☎ 01371 859259. Towards the end of the walk you reach the Cricketers, a traditional pub serving down-to-earth bar food and snacks with two real ales on tap. It is closed on Monday lunchtimes. ☎ 01371 873359.

The Walk

❶ Leave the car park to walk past the church and between delightful houses, back to the main road. Go right, passing the **Angel and Harp**, to go left in front of a small green. Pass a five-bar gate and follow a surfaced path across a playing field. Keep forward at a junction to go between hedges and through gates to the road.

❷ Turn left. Cross and go right at the roundabout to walk a few yards up **The Downs** to go left on grass, now with houses to your left and an old wall to the right. Keep forward to reach an ornamental lake – from this position you have an attractive view across **Great Dunmow**. Turn right to join a path by a dog bin to pass an ornamental bench installed by the Women's Institute. Just before the road, go left up past a play area and tennis court to go through a car park to the road.

Summer

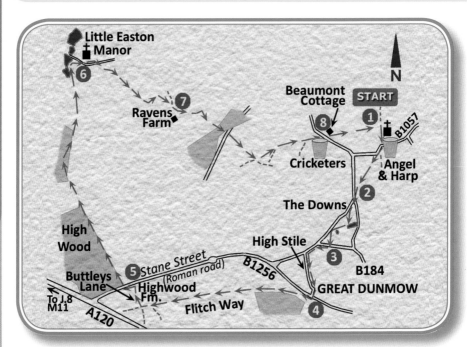

3 Go right, cross and fork left at the roundabout. Go left along **High Stile** and, where this swings left, keep forward between barriers. Now follow the pathway, always downhill to reach steps and a road.

4 Cross carefully to climb steps slightly to the left on the other side. At the top turn sharply right. Keep forward, ignoring all side paths, sometimes using board-walks and passing under a bridge, for nearly a mile. Eventually you arrive at a double-gated cross-track (**Buttleys Lane**); go right, passing **Highwood Farm**, to emerge on **Stane Street** – part of a famous Roman road.

5 Cross and go left. Just before **High Wood**, go right at a bridleway sign along the left edge of a field. Keep forward for about ½ mile; when you go under power lines, swing right with the track and continue after the next field boundary. Now the woodland has been replaced by a hedge. Keep to the left, alongside the hedge, as you approach the hamlet of **Little Easton Manor**. Take a fenced path on the left and almost immediately go left through a gap in the fence. Fork right down to the lake then right up the bank to exit by a gate. (You may want to explore further here – the owners of the Rectory allow access.)

6 Walk towards the church (this and Little Easton Manor are well worth a visit – the former houses old wall paintings, two windows dedicated to American servicemen, brasses, and numerous massive monuments, some dating back to the 15th century, featuring the ancestors of the Countess of Warwick). When you leave, walk up the drive with the church to your left, passing an estate house with the prominent Warwick symbol, dated 1895. Go right at a concrete fingerpost. Immediately fork left. Keep left of trees surrounding a pond and go forward on a well-defined cross-field path. (This flat area was sought for the expansion of Stansted Airport.) At the field boundary go sharp left at a waymarker on a path, which gradually veers to the right to approach **Ravens Farm**. Cross a drive and join a concrete track.

7 Keep forward (possibly accompanied by guinea fowl). Go left under power lines in front of a house then go right at a waymarker along its perimeter fence to continue into a strip of woodland, over a stream and up a bank to a road. Cross and go up the bank opposite, going left to pick up a footpath, which goes right through a gap in the fence. Continue uphill with trees and a chain fence to the left. (This area is due for development so the path is subject to re-routing.) At the top of the rise go left at a waymarker (now you can appreciate the massive expansion of Great Dunmow in recent years). Keep forward with a leisure centre and school over to the left. Continue along the backs of gardens. The path eventually curves left, past a redundant stile, to a drive, which you

The old railway line.

cross onto a green. Go diagonally right, to the left of a pond, towards the **Cricketers pub**. Reach a road.

8 Cross and walk down beside the pub to turn left, after **Beaumont Cottage**, along a narrow path to reach a field, which you cross diagonally right to return to the car park.

What to look out for –

If you had stumbled across the **Flitch Way** at stage 4 of this walk by accident, you would be hard pressed at first to realise that this was once a railway trackbed. Later, the raised embankment, the cuttings and the bridge would have given the clues you needed but the years since the line was decommissioned in 1972 have shown how completely and comparatively quickly nature can regain its territory. Built by the Victorians and opened in 1869, this 15-mile route from Bishop's Stortford to Braintree brought prosperity to the area – on its demise it became a country park.

The isolation from farmed areas means that the unimproved nature of the soil encourages the growth of a wide range of wild flowering plants, especially on the southern bank of the Dunmow cutting, which you will walk on this route. Late spring provides banks of cowslips, which are replaced during summer by oxeye daisies, wild sweet peas, vetch, scabious, orchids, buttercups and many others.

The name of the path derives from the ancient four-yearly Flitch Ceremony (mentioned in Chaucer's *Canterbury Tales*), originating in Little Dunmow and now celebrated by its great brother. It involved giving a flitch, a large piece of bacon, to a couple who had not repented of marriage after a year and a day.

7 Fyfield

The path bordering the Roding.

Very soon after leaving Fyfield you will cross the Roding. It is hard to appreciate that this sedate and attractive river can cause so much havoc downstream in Redbridge when it occasionally floods. You will pick up the riverside several times on the return journey but for now you will continue along quiet woodland edges, passing some glorious houses, to reach the small village of Willingale. Unusually for Essex, this route crosses several meadows that display the flowers enhancing the field edges in the spring and early summer.

35

Distance 5½ miles.

Terrain This is an easy walk along quiet lanes and field edges. It is particularly well signed. In high summer, when there has been a lack of rain, the surface of parts of the route can become hard and cracked.

Map OS Explorer 183 Chelmsford & The Rodings.

Starting point Roadside parking along the road that runs south from the B184 in Fyfield, starting alongside the telephone kiosk and village sign between the post office and the Queen's Head (GR TL570069).

How to get there Fyfield is on the B184, the road that runs between Chipping Ongar and Great Dunmow. This can be accessed from the M11 via the A414.

Refreshments The Queen's Head, which is open every day, has developed an enviable reputation locally as a dining pub, and it always has at least three well-kept ales. There is an inviting main menu but also a delicious range of sandwiches and traditional Essex huffers. ☎ 01277 899231.

The Walk

1 Walk away from the main road and continue, swinging left over a bridge and the **River Roding**. Pass the **church of St Nicholas** and the top of **Cannon's Lane** to go left of the drive to **Fyfield Grange**. The footpath soon leads onto a gravel walkway through a tasteful development. Cross a wide drive to a waymarker in front of a hedge. Turn right, walking with the hedge on the left and passing the end of a line of conifers. Pass more conifers and go right along the field edge, going left at the corner. Towards the end of the field, continue, to the right of a house, along a hedged path to join a drive and reach a lane.

2 Go left and then right through a gate to the left of the drive to **Witney Green**. Go diagonally left to another gate (you are now on the **Essex Way**). Follow the red poppy symbols across this and the next field then cross a bridge to a road. Turn left. Go straight forward across the junction, along **Miller's Green Road**, and immediately go right over a bridge and then left along the field edge. The path traces the boundary of a house. Look for a waymarker in the hedge then go right across the field and over a bridge. Go left and follow the field edge to go right up the field with the hedge to the left. At the end, cross a bridge

The magnificent Duke's farmhouse at point 3 of the route.

and go right towards two churches – walk between them to reach a road.

3 Turn left to walk through the village of **Willingale**. Before the road bends to the right, go left at a concrete fingerpost along gravel to the left of a garage. Emerge from a dark, hedged path on the left edge of a field. Follow the edge around right to reach a road. Go left (notice **Duke's Farmhouse** to the right). Look for a footpath left, just before **McKerros.** Follow the right edge of the field along the perimeter of the house grounds. Continue along the banks of the **River Roding**, flowing so gently here. Cross a narrow green into the next field and continue on the right edge. Eventually cross a concrete bridge to a lane.

4 Cross and go down steps and along the right edge of the field. Turn right at

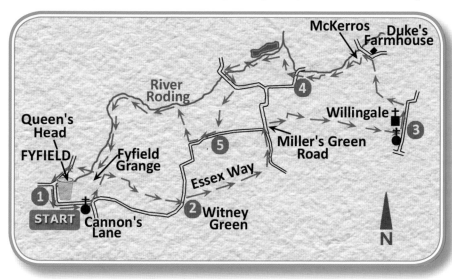

Summer

37

a waymarker to cross a bridge and go left. Go right over the next bridge and go forward to a waymarker towards the end of the hedge. Turn left at right-angles and head towards a gate in the distance (when I was here there was no path visible on the ground). Go through a V-stile to a lane. Turn left, crossing **Gang Bridge**. Go right at a fingerpost. Keep forward, at first parallel to a wooden fence, then across this and the next field. Reach a gate and road.

5 Turn right. On the corner of the road go right at a concrete fingerpost across the middle of the field. At the boundary, go left along the river, ignoring a metal bridge on the right. On approaching a wooden fence, jutting out, your path crosses the corner of the field and continues with a hedge on the left. Continue through a gap in a fence and, just before housing, cross a bridge on the right. Take the left fork across the field and to the left of a hedge to a stile and road. Cross to the pavement and turn left. At the junction go left and return to your car.

What to look out for –

When you enter the village of Willingale at the end of stage 2 it will probably be the only time that you pass between **two churches that share a single churchyard**. The local legend is that two sisters owned the original church. They had a furious row about who should sit where in the front pew with the result that one of them, the

richest, decided to build her own church alongside. Attractive as this tale is, it is rather undermined by the fact that one church is 200 years older than the other!

The real history is a bit more prosaic. Research has shown that, originally, Willingale comprised two parishes: Spain and Doe. Harvey D'Espania built the church of Willingale Spain, giving his name to the parish, in the 12th century. In the 14th century, when wool production was flourishing, the D'ou family came to live in the area; they financed a new church to cater for the increasing population. The two parishes were united in 1929. Now St Christopher's, formerly of Doe, is the parish church whilst St Andrews and All Saints', previously Spain, is used for special occasions.

8 Canvey Island

Looking across the water from Canvey.

This is a short and very easy walk based on a new RSPB nature reserve and is included here to inveigle those who have never been to Canvey Island to visit and to later explore other routes and learn more about Canvey's history.

We walk out to a section of the sea wall which is just part of an exciting 16-mile route which circles the whole of the island. On the return we visit all three hides of the reserve which overlook lakes teeming with waterfowl. Two picnic areas provide opportunities to take a break. At the end of the tour of the reserve, advantage is taken of the location to visit the famous Dutch House.

39

Distance 3¾ miles.

Terrain All the paths are surfaced except for the short section along the sea wall. Thus, most of the walk is pushchair and wheelchair friendly. Please be aware, though, that if you do the walk during the winter or spring, some sections of the path are liable to flooding.

Map OS Explorer 175 Southend-on-Sea & Basildon.

Starting point The large, free RSPB car park (GR TQ775842).

How to get there Cross to the island by either the B104 or A130. At the first roundabout continue on the A130 to a second one; the car park is a turning right off this.

Refreshments There are none on the walk but Canvey is a seaside resort so there are plenty of cafés and pubs along the seafront. You might like to try the Lobster Smack which is some distance away from the main entertainment area, is open all day, and prides itself on having 'the best value pub grub in the area'. ☎ 01268 514297. The pub, which was known to Charles Dickens who mentioned it in *Great Expectations,* is housed in a Grade II listed building dating to the 17th century. To reach it from the car park, continue on the A130 over two roundabouts to turn right on Haven Road.

The Walk

❶ Walk toward the main entrance of the car park, going right to a metal kissing-gate to immediately join a surfaced path which, for a time, runs parallel to the road with a ditch to the left. Continue with the path as it swings away to the right and continues around a collection of small ponds. Reach a junction with a fingerpost.

❷ Keep forward with a ditch to the right to arrive at another junction. Go left. The path twists, turns and crosses a stream. Eventually you come to a bank on the right with an information board and a couple of seats. (From the top you can get a good view of **South Benfleet** and, further to the right, of **Hadleigh Castle**). Continue. (Now, ahead, you can see the fractionating columns of **Shell Haven**, on the other side of the estuary from Canvey. If the day is dull you may also see waste gas being burnt off.) The path swings right to cross a more substantial ditch, then through a kissing gate to join a tree-lined path. Reach another signposted junction.

3 Keep forward. Soon after the hedge finishes, you will pass **Pantile Farm** picnic area on the left. Continue through a kissing gate and up a bank to the sea wall.

4 Turn right to walk along the sea wall until just before another gate; descend the bank and go through a kissing-gate by a fingerpost to re-enter the reserve. Join a surfaced path to reach the first of three hides on the left. Soon the path swings to the right to arrive at a T-junction. Go left here, repeating a section of your outward journey. At the next path junction go left to the second hide and three windmills. (These windmills are probably used to pump excess water.) Retrace your steps.

Summer

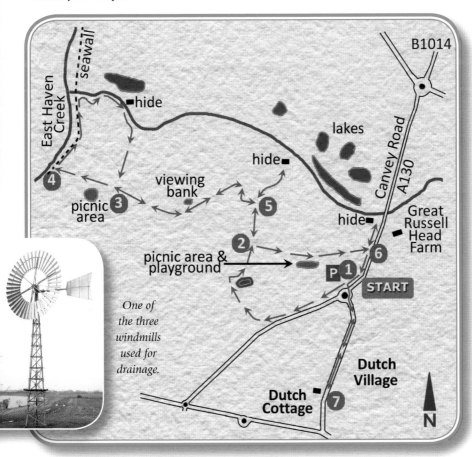

B1014

East Haven Creek · seawall

■hide

lakes

hide■

viewing bank

picnic **3** area

4

5

hide■

Canvey Road A130

Great Russell Head Farm

picnic area & playground

2

6

P **1**

START

One of the three windmills used for drainage.

Dutch Village

Dutch Cottage

7

N

5 At the junction turn left and go left again at the next junction, passing a children's playground. Reach a T-junction.

6 Go left to a third hide. Retrace your steps and keep forward at the junction. You will be walking parallel with the road to the car park. Leave by the main entrance and walk, with care, across the centre of the roundabout. Go left on the verge and follow this around, with the road, to the right. After less than ¼ mile turn right down a path signed as a dead-end, passing between bollards to visit the **Dutch House**.

7 Retrace your steps to the car park.

What to look out for –

Canvey was originally made up of five separate islands in the Thames Estuary. These were mainly marshlands supporting only sheep and shepherds. In the 17th century Canvey Island was drained and a sea wall was built by the Dutch engineer Cornelius Vermuyden. His workers from the Netherlands brought with them their  families who settled on the island and they built rather unusual octagonal cottages of which two still survive. The one visited on this walk, the **Dutch House,** is the oldest, bearing the date 1618.

Whilst the land was successfully drained, it was always subject to flooding and in 1953 the North Sea flood devastated the island costing the lives of 58 people, and led to the temporary evacuation of the 13,000 residents. Since then Canvey has been protected by modern sea defences comprising 15 miles of concrete sea wall and various barrages.

You can visit the grounds of the Dutch House at any time. The museum which it contains is open from Spring Bank Holiday to September between 2.30 pm and 5 pm, on Wednesdays and Sundays and between 10 am and l pm and 2 pm to 5 pm on Bank Holidays. ☎ 01268 753487.

⟳ ⑨ Great Sampford

The moat at Maynards.

This is an ideal walk for a hot summer's day. You amble along the cool sides of shady woods, soon gazing across the Pant valley at the charming scene of Little Sampford church nestling in a tree-clothed hamlet. Here there are quiet meadows that seem out of time, disturbed only by the whine of insects feeding on the flowers. The return, along the banks of the Pant, will also feature insects dancing on the waters and the occasional splash of the fish that feed on them. The countryside, especially during the second half, is untamed enough to cause you to concentrate on the route from time to time – hopefully, this will just add to your enjoyment.

Distance 6 miles.

Terrain Paths on the first part of the walk are usually quite well maintained. They are mainly along field edges and quiet country lanes. The return journey is more difficult and will require strict attention to the directions. It would be useful if a map reader was a member of your party.

Map OS Explorer 195 Braintree & Saffron Walden.

Starting point Homebridge, a residential road with roadside parking, opposite the Red Lion pub in Great Sampford (GR TL 644354).

How to get there Great Sampford is a rather difficult place to get to. It is probably best to take the B1057, which runs between Haverhill and Great Dunmow, and then turn off at Finchingfield on the B1053. This road meets the B1051 in Great Sampford just beyond the Red Lion. If approaching via the B1051, find the major road junction and take the road opposite the church.

Refreshments The Red Lion, opposite the parking place, is an unpretentious and comfortable village pub. There is a good range of snacks and a surprisingly wide variety of more substantial meals. ☎ 01799 586325.

The Walk

❶ Walk back to the main road and turn right, following it round at the junction. Opposite a barn, go left through a six-bar gate and along the left of an old garage then the lower edge of a garden with a stream to the left. Emerge at a field corner and continue along the left edge of this and the next field. At the field boundary, go right up to the road.

❷ Cross and go forward to the right of a line of conifers and, where this ends, continue under power lines to reach the field boundary. Go left with a ditch to the right. Pass the field boundary on the right and soon look for a plank bridge over the ditch. Cross to the far left-hand corner of the ornamental meadow and exit by an earth bridge. Turn right along a field edge, now with a hedge and a moat to your right, to reach a lane.

❸ Turn right, passing **Maynards**; you are now walking amid a Roadside

Nature Reserve. Continue along this lane for just over ½ mile. After passing the unprepossessing **Mount Hall**, go left at a fingerpost along a drive, which you leave to keep forward to the far left-hand corner of the field. Go through a gap and go right along a field edge. Pass under power lines and go left at the field boundary. Turn right at a waymarker to walk alongside a wood, **Bliss Grove**, and then continue along a wide grassy track. Veer right at the next boundary, keeping the hedge on your left and continue to a road.

④ Immediately go sharp left to leave the road along the right edge of a field. Cross a bridge in the corner to walk alongside **Little Almond's Grove**, cross a track and continue with **Long Almond's Grove** on the left. Reach a hedge, which is jutting out, and go left before it along a track to the right of a ditch. Arrive at a junction of tracks and go right into woodland, continuing to reach the road.

⑤ Turn right for about ¼ mile. Come to the **Garland's Farm** complex on the left. After passing a barn go left alongside an open wooden fence and continue along the left field edge to reach a gap and bridge in the far left corner. Keep to the left in the next two fields, gradually descending the valley side. At the bottom ignore a path to the left and a track to the right to go forward over a plank bridge.

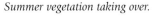

Summer vegetation taking over.

Summer

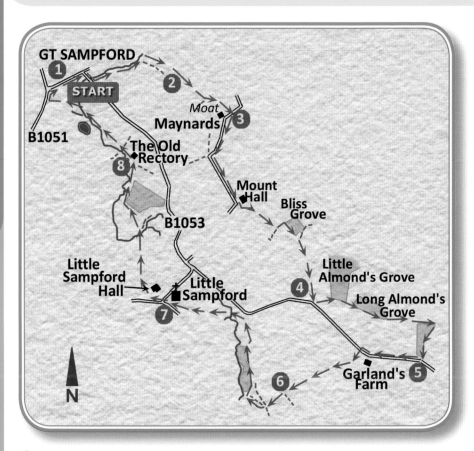

6 Keep forward to the **River Pant** and turn right to walk along its bank. Reach a concrete track with a bridge to the left; turn right, following the woodland edge as it eventually swings left at a waymarker. At the end of the field go right with a ditch and trees to the left and go left at a waymarker over an earth bridge. Walk along the right edge of the field to a waymarker alongside a barn (here classic cars are restored – if you are lucky you may see some parked in the front). Turn left here to a prominent bridge. Cross the bridge and walk up the centre of the field. Cross a stile to enter a paddock and another to enter the churchyard of **St Mary the Virgin** in **Little Sampford**. Go left alongside the boundary of a garden to a road.

7 Turn right then fork left at a junction. Go right along the drive to **Little Sampford Hall** to keep forward between farm buildings with the Hall well over to the right. Go through a seven-bar gate alongside a bungalow and immediately cross a stile on the right. Go straight across the field to another stile then keep forward to a gated bridge to the right of a clump of trees ahead. Maintain your direction along a raised field boundary; after a tree, swing right to a stile. Once over, go forward towards the **Millfield Plantation** – gradually veering left to walk beside it. At the end swing right to continue along the edge of the wood and then a hedge. When the hedge swings sharply left, look to the right for a stile (ahead is the **Old Rectory**).

8 Turn left along the edge of a meadow and continue with this and the river to reach a stile. Keep to the left edge of the next field, ignoring a concrete bridge to later cross a bridge/stile combination. Now head slightly diagonally right to the left edge of a wood ahead. Join a wide track alongside the Pant. Pass a weir on the left and turn away from the river. Once under power lines, go left through a gap in the hedge over a plank bridge. Turn right along the hedge for a short distance. Go left into the field on a clear path then fork left to reach the road. Go right and turn right opposite the church to return to your car.

What to look out for –

As you start along the road past **Maynards** at stage 3, you join a **Roadside Nature Reserve**. These special verges are usually designated with markers. This one-mile section is part of the 27 miles of these little-known nature reserves in Essex. Careful management ensures that a wide variety of plants, including rare species, are conserved and are able to thrive. This, in turn, benefits butterflies and other insects, small mammals and birds, providing them with food and shelter. Roadside verges are also important in linking isolated habitats providing 'wildlife corridors' that enable animals to move between 'islands'. Some of the species that are recorded at the Maynards verges are cowslip in the spring, followed among others by red campion, yellow archangel, pellitory-of-the-wall, bush vetch and ribbed melilot.

10 Danbury

Riffhams, seen across the fields.

This summer walk is the equivalent, in rambling terms, to one of those taster menus served in posh restaurants. It gives you a brief experience of three different landscapes, all on the borders of Danbury. The country park is the residue of an estate dominated by the palace; it has lakes, formal gardens and rolling meadows. Lingwood Common, high to the north of the town, is more densely wooded and its undulations offer something of a roller-coaster ride. The walk finishes with Danbury Common, which, although wooded, has many of the characteristics of heathland. Each of these areas could easily offer a separate day's outing so I hope that you will be tempted to return and explore for yourself.

Distance 5 miles.

Terrain Paths are generally very good; even where there is mud it can generally be avoided. Parts are quite hilly, especially Lingwood Common.

Map OS Explorer 183 Chelmsford & The Rodings.

Starting point The free National Trust car park at GR TL782044 on Danbury Common.

How to get there Approaching via the A12, take the A414 eastwards to Danbury and then the first turning right at a mini-roundabout to the west of the town. Turn left at the bottom of the hill to go along Woodhill Road and Bicknacre Road. Just after passing Plumptre Lane on the right, turn left on an unsigned drive to the car park.

Refreshments You will pass the Cricketers Arms at the start of stage 7. The pub is open every day (12 noon to 8.30 pm on Sundays). Fish is a particular feature at lunchtimes. Home-made cakes and tea and coffee are also available from 9.30 am until 4.30 pm on Monday to Saturday. ☎ 01245 222022.

The Walk

① Leave the car park and return to the road. Turn right and then left along **Plumptre Lane**. Where the houses finish at a T-junction, go left and then swing right and right again at a fork. Just past **Ludgores Farm** the drive swings right to a lane where you go left and soon fork right. Ignore a footpath through the hedge to the right and a little later keep left alongside a line of houses to pass some small bollards and join a narrow path. Keep to this path until it eventually emerges on a road.

② Cross diagonally left to go through a 'no entry' gap into a car park. Walk left to an information board (there are seasonal lavatories to the right). Go through the barrier and take the path that goes from the board and initially curves slightly towards the road. At a maroon-topped post go left and continue straight on at the next to enter and cross a second car park and picnic area. Keep forward so that you are now walking alongside a lake. Keep forward, ignoring a path to the right, to pass a second lake. Pass to the right of lavatories (open all year round) and fork left towards the bottom of a slope to fork right again

Summer

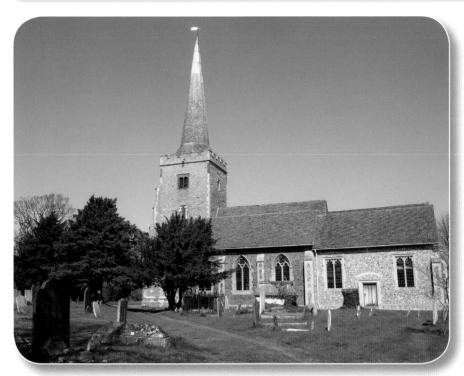

Danbury church is a Grade 1 listed building.

around a third, smaller pond. Now walk uphill alongside a beech hedge on your left. Join a surfaced path, which swings right through formal gardens. Keep forward at a fork (if you go left here you can get a glimpse of **Danbury Palace**) to continue on the path nearest to the lakes. Avoid the right turn between the lakes; almost at the end of the water, turn left at a red and blue topped post.

3 Keep forward across a meadow to a gate and fingerpost. Follow the wide, grassy track indicated by the fingerpost and take an early right fork to keep with it. Join a stony track coming in from the right (the palace is over to the left) and arrive at a lonely waymarker set in a spacious junction. Go hard right to the first of a series of waymarkers on a winding path, through woodland and across a meadow, to a road.

4 Cross to walk up **Riffhams Lane**. At a junction with Elm Green Lane, go left over a stile. Go forward over this glorious meadow with **Riffhams** set in the hill on the right. Pass to the left of a pond and, once over the brow, you can see the next stile ahead. Continue into woodland (past what looks like double stocks).

Keep forward to emerge and walk with a fence to the left (over to your left you have extensive views of Chelmsford). Cross a stile to a lane.

5 Go right. Fork left at the junction and then go right along a track (on the **Admiral McHardy Way**). Keep forward at the sign for **Lingwood Common**. Eventually, after ¹/₃ mile, you will pass a blue bridleway sign to the right; ignore this and go up the slope ahead where there is a bench at cross-tracks. After your rest, go right downhill on a narrower path. Fork right at a wooden fence and continue, now on a surfaced drive, which later climbs steeply between houses to a road.

Summer

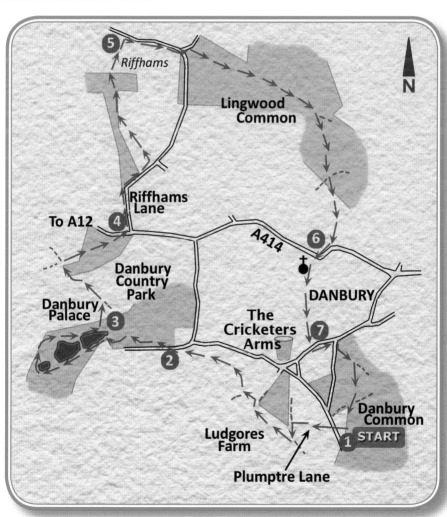

6 Turn right and cross towards the church, which you pass on a track to the left. At the end, all the climbing is rewarded by a panoramic view. Take the broad path straight down the hill, through a gate to a lane.

7 Go left (the **Cricketers Arms** is a few yards to the right), walking on the right-hand verge. Go right at the road junction and quickly left at an open access sign. Ignore a narrow path to the right but, at the next junction, with a short blue waymarker, go right. Keep with the main path until you see the car park over to your right.

What to look out for –

Stage 5 of the walk, through Lingwood Common, briefly joins the **Admiral McHardy Way**, which commemorates John McHardy who, in Clowes' *History of the British Navy*, is referred to as being 'the terror equally of pirates and of slavers in the West Indies'. As acting lieutenant aboard the *Icarus*, he was involved in the capture off Havana of the pirate schooner *Diableto*. Later, in 1829, as captain of *The Pickle*, he famously captured a slave ship, *Boladora*. After leaving the  navy as an Admiral, McHardy became the first and longest-serving Chief Constable of the Essex Police from 1840–1881. The McHardy Way, a 10-mile walk, was dedicated to the founding father of the Essex Police to commemorate 150 years of the force.

Danbury Palace, passed during stage 2 occupies a site near an earlier, 15th-century, house called Danbury Place. It was built in the 1830s and was sold to the church as a home for the Bishop of Rochester – since then it has been known as a 'palace'. It was used as a maternity hospital in the Second World War and then as an educational establishment. It has now been developed into apartments.

11 Epping – Copped Hall

Majestic beech trees in the forest.

Whilst Epping Forest is beautiful at any time of the year, it is, for me, at its best in the autumn when the leaves have begun falling to reveal the majestic shapes of the ancient coppiced beeches. This walk largely eschews the drives, the surfaced paths prepared specifically for the horse-riders, which criss-cross the Forest. Early on we have to find our way over indistinct paths and along infrequently walked routes to go under the motorway by a tunnel known only to local walkers. Later, during a gentle climb, we have a very real chance of seeing deer before emerging from trees to superb views across the surrounding countryside. Our return takes us past Copped Hall, which is being restored. You may like to return in the early summer to see the rhododendrons flowering on the final stage of the walk.

Distance 3¼ miles.

Terrain There are climbs and descents on this walk but both are gradual. The first half of the walk is on narrow paths that can be muddy after rain. Take particular care at the start of section 2 and just after the beginning of section 3 that you are on the correct route – the remainder is easy to follow.

Map OS Explorer 174 Epping Forest & Lee Valley.

Starting point A small unmarked parking area, by a bus stop, with a height barrier on the western side of the B1393 between the Wakes Arms roundabout (now with the Old Orleans on its site) and the traffic lights to the south of Epping (GR TL431998).

How to get there Leave the M25 at junction 26 and take the A121 towards Loughton. At the roundabout (with the Old Orleans pub) turn left on the B1393. The parking area is about ¹/₃ mile along on the left next to a bus stop.

Refreshments Near to the parking area, on the roundabout, is the Old Orleans (☎ 01992 812618); this is a restaurant with an emphasis on Cajun cooking and is an excellent venue if you have children with you. Upshire, which can be reached by taking the next turning left from the parking area, has two very good but more conventional pubs, both along the main road: the Good Intent (☎ 01992 712066) and the Horseshoes (☎ 01992 712745).

The Walk

❶ Walk towards the main road from the parking area then go right, before the road, on a surfaced ride. Descend a dip to cross a seasonal stream and walk up the other side, looking for a post bearing an indistinct horseshoe on the right. Now follow white-topped posts at irregular intervals but roughly in a straight line downhill. (If you have children with you, it will be a challenge for them to spot the 'next post' – there are 7 in all.) Continue to the edge of the wood at the bottom of the slope; ahead is a ditch and open country.

❷ Look to your right for some old concrete fencing posts; after finding these you should discover another horseshoe-marker post. Walk up the slope to this

Deer spotted crossing the fields.

post and the path alongside it and, after a few yards, go left at a fork. You should be walking near the boundary of the woodland and you should be able to see open land and more concrete fencing posts on the left between the trees (if you can see open land on both sides – you are on the wrong path). Cross a stream early on and climb gradually, always in view of the boundary to reach a drive by **Poacher's Meet**. Continue to a road.

3 Cross and walk left downhill at a post on a track through the trees. About 25 yards before reaching a clearing at the bottom of the slope, go right and climb a low bank and walk forward (there is no path) to pick up another path going downhill and turn left. At the bottom of the hill this path swings right with a waymarker. If all has gone well you should be on a path within a relatively narrow sliver of woodland. Through the trees on both sides is open land and ahead is the M25. Go through a tunnel under the motorway.

4 On the other side, swing right uphill for a few yards then turn left; do not cross the stile ahead. You are now walking along another corridor of trees. Below, to the left, is a lively brook whilst over to the right you will get your first views of **Copped Hall** and, very likely, some deer. Reach a wooden fence and go to the right of a house through a kissing-gate (to the right here you can get an excellent view of the Hall). Follow the line of the fence to reach a drive.

5 Turn right, keeping forward past some rather grand houses (the public access notice refers to motor vehicles). Continue forward at a junction but when the drive swings right, descend across grass to a gap in the hedge ahead. Cross a bridge into a field and go forward, aiming for a point just right of the house on the horizon where you will find a stile. Cross and go right to a drive.

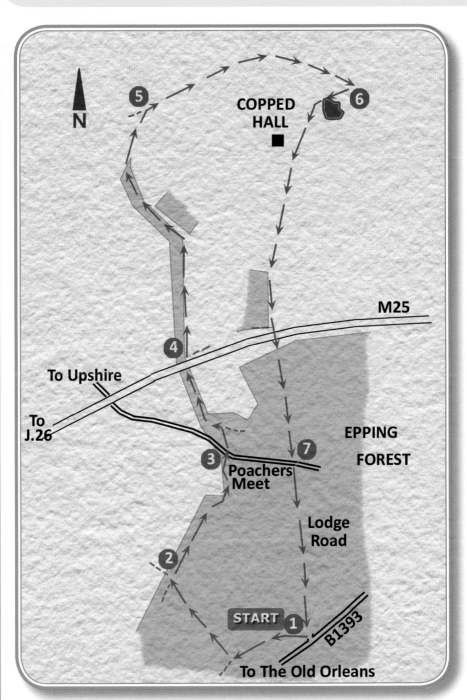

Autumn

N

⑤

COPPED
HALL

⑥

M25

To Upshire

To
J.26

④

③

Poachers
Meet

⑦

EPPING

FOREST

Lodge
Road

②

START ①

B1393

To The Old Orleans

6 Go right, pass a pond (I have seen terrapins sunning themselves here in the summer), and go left besides a gate on a track to the left. Walk past **Copped Hall** and continue along its drive to cross the motorway. The drive, which was bisected by the motorway, maintains its direction to reach the gates to the Hall. Leave by the small gate on the right to reach the road.

7 Cross and go forward. (You are now on **Lodge Road**, which was only closed to traffic in the mid 1990s; it is a good demonstration of the speed at which Nature can reclaim its own.) Keep forward; just before the main road you will reach the parking area on the right.

What to look out for –

If you have noticed **Copped Hall** when driving along the M25, from which it dominates the skyline, you could be forgiven for believing you are viewing the home of landed gentry. The reality is that Copped Hall was virtually destroyed by fire in 1917 and what the motorist observes now is a shell. Built in the mid-18th century the present building replaced an earlier one that was, at times, owned by Henry VIII and Elizabeth I. When the M25 was built it was routed, against much local opposition, right through the middle of the Copped Hall Estate. One result of this development was that the site of the house and grounds became a target for speculators. From 1986–1995 a campaign was successfully fought by a few dedicated individuals against repeated large-scale aggressive development proposals for the mansion and parkland. A Trust was set up and volunteers are gradually restoring the building and its gardens; a marvellous act of faith which few of them, if any, will see completed in their lifetime. The website www.coppedhalltrust.org.uk will tell you more.

12 Belchamp St Paul

Autumn

The start of the walk.

This is an unpretentious walk for autumn when the crops have been harvested and the cross-field paths are clear. There is time for contemplation here; along the quiet lanes that link two of the Belchamps – those of Otten and St Paul. The origin of the name 'Belchamp' is variously given as 'beau champs', meaning beautiful fields, or 'bylcham', meaning beamed roofs; both are equally applicable. The 'St Paul' part of the name is because the parish was given to St Paul's Cathedral in the year AD931 and remained largely ecclesiastical property until 1947, whilst 'Otten' derives from the family of Otto who owned the village in the early 12th century. Unusually for such a short walk in the depths of the country, we pass three lovely pubs – this, along with plentiful birdsong and a great variety of flowering plants, may tempt you back again in the summer.

The Facts

Distance 4½ miles.

Terrain An easy walk with gentle gradients along lanes and across fields (these may be muddy after heavy rain).

Maps OS Explorers 210 Newmarket & Haverhill and 196 Sudbury, Hadleigh & Dedham Vale.

Starting point The telephone kiosk at the junction in the centre of Belchamp St Paul. There are no specified parking areas here but roadside parking is permitted (GR TL792423).

How to get there Belchamp St Paul is signed off the A1017, which runs between Haverhill and Sible Hedingham, at Great Yeldham.

Refreshments The Half Moon, at the start of the walk, is the quintessential village pub: 16th-century, overlooking the village green, hanging baskets, thatched roof, leaded windows, low beams and a real log fire when needed. It serves good food and real ales; note though that it is closed on Mondays. ☎ 01787 277402. Also available are the Cherry Tree Inn at Knowl Green (☎ 01787 237263) and the Red Lion at Belchamp Otten (☎ 01787 278301).

The Walk

❶ Walk along the green with the village sign on the right and the **Half Moon** public house on the left. Continue almost to the end of the green verge and then turn right at a concrete fingerpost. Cross the field diagonally right to a kissing-gate then go forward, across the next field, continuing alongside a hedge to a corner. Go over a plank bridge crossing the next field to reach a vague field boundary.

❷ Go left (if you go under power lines you've gone too far). A reassuring waymarker encourages you to the end of the field where you swing right on a narrow field-edge path (the path should cut a corner but it wasn't reinstated when I was last here), which you follow to eventually reach a gap in a corner. Walk, slightly right, across the next field to go down steps and cross a bridge. Follow a fenced section to a lane.

❸ Turn left to enter **Knowl Green**. At the crossroads go left along **Gage's Road**.

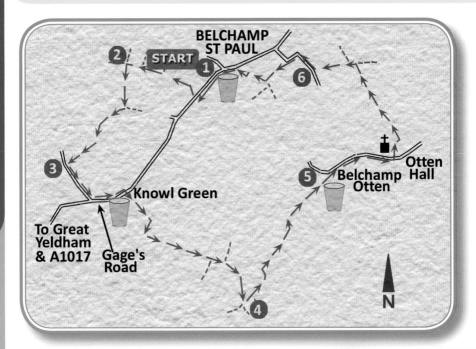

Pass the **Cherry Tree Inn**, go over a bridge and turn right at a fingerpost. You are now on a wide grassy track, which swings right in the next field. At the end, go slightly left to cross a bridge and turn left. Continue on the left edge of the next field after crossing a plank bridge and keep forward to pass a clearing with a concrete standing on the left. Soon you will come to two bridges; cross the first.

The church at point 5 of the walk.

4 Cross a concrete farm track and walk up the field. About a third of the way up, look for a left fork and follow this to another concrete track and a field corner. (This fork is easily missed; if you carry straight on you can pick up the concrete track and follow it back around left to the corner.) Go through a gap in the hedge onto a sunken path, which emerges on the right edge of a field. Continue on a hedged path, which feeds into a lane passing the **Red Lion** to reach a road.

5 Go right into **Belchamp Otten** where there are some particularly attractive houses and the charming **church of St Ethelbert and All Saints**. (This church is well worth a visit; basically Norman, it has had many additions and renovations – of particular interest are the Jacobean pulpit, the Queen Ann altar rails and the small Georgian gallery.) Once past the church, ignore a concrete track, then turn left on a gravel drive to walk between a lake on the left and **Otten Hall** on the right. Go through a gate in the wall and forward across a yard. Turn right between barns and keep forward to go through a small metal gate. At the end of the fence on the left, turn left on a wide track along the field edge. Towards the end of the field go diagonally left to cross a plank bridge. Go straight across the next field. At the next boundary, cross a plank bridge and continue with a hedge on the left. Cross a three-plank bridge and go left, soon forking left to continue with a hedge on the right. Reach a lane.

6 Turn right. Go around a left-hand bend then keep forward on a wide, hedged track at the next bend. Where the track swings left, go right on a field-edge path. Waymarkers take you alongside a school and back to the road on which you parked your car.

What to look out for –

Most of the villages in this book will have at least one or two houses with a **thatched roof** and you may be fortunate enough to see a **thatcher** at work during your walk. To become a thatcher entails an apprenticeship of two to five years. Whilst it is claimed that thatch is cool in summer and warm in winter, thatch for new houses is rare, probably because of the expense of its maintenance. Many thatched houses are listed and it is important to ensure that the style of thatch and materials used are in the spirit of the traditions of the local area, as well as complying with the requirements of English  Heritage or the local council. Areas have their own idiosyncrasies: North Essex, for instance, has pinnacles, which were supposed to ward off evil spirits, incorporated into the roof. Historically, wheat straw was used but nowadays water reed is the preferred material. The thatch is fixed in place by hazel or steel staples. The bulk of the roof can last for 75 years although it will need re-ridging every 10 to 15 years – this is why the ridges of thatched houses often look much newer than the rest of the roof.

13 Fordham

The magnificent West Bergholt Hall.

This is a walk for autumn mornings when the air is cool and clear. The Fordham Hall Estate is, at 505 acres, one of the largest undertakings by the Woodland Trust. At the time of writing, the planting of thousands of trees is relatively new – in time it will become a truly important recreational area. Although this walk will venture into the estate, the route concentrates on following a section of the River Colne along its valley, making use of the Essex Way for the outward journey. We do enter a more 'traditional' Woodland Trust property, Hillhouse Wood, which is quite remarkable, mainly for its crop of bluebells but also for the rich flora at other times of the year, which results from the mosaic of woodland types.

There are other highlights: we divert to visit the 18th-century Cook's Mill alongside the Colne and later pass by West Bergholt Hall, a much grander affair of three storeys, also 18th-century.

The Facts

Distance 6½ miles.

Terrain The Colne valley is relatively shallow so there are few gradients. Most of the paths are good but expect some mud after heavy rain. The route uses some permissive paths and also provides a couple of opportunities to make your own way on access land but you can keep to recognised paths if you so wish.

Map OS Explorer 184 Colchester, Harwich & Clacton-on-Sea.

Starting point The free car park at one of the entrances to the Woodland Trust's Fordham Hall Estate (GR TL928286).

How to get there Fordham is north-west of Colchester between the B1508 and the A1124. The car park is at its north end off Ponders Road.

Refreshments Midway around the walk, 50 yards off the route, is the Shoulder of Mutton at Fordstreet. It has three well-kept Shepherd Neame beers and a menu of excellent pub fare. There is a spacious riverside garden for dining alfresco. No food on Mondays. ☎ 01206 240464. In Fordham, near to the church at the southern end of the village, is the Three Horseshoes, which offers a good bar menu during the week and massive Sunday roasts. Open all day except for Mondays. ☎ 01206 240195.

The Walk

1 With your back to the car park entrance, go to the right-hand field boundary and turn left to follow the hedge on the right. Continue, going diagonally left along the field edge at the first corner, later ignoring a bridge on the right. Pass a nesting-box perched on a tall pole and walk with a strip of woodland to your right. At a waymarker, descend through the trees to the right to cross a bridge and go left along a field edge.

2 You are now on a permissive path. Keep the stream to your left, ignoring cross-paths, until, towards the end of the second field, you cross a bridge with a hand-rail on the left. Almost immediately, cross right, through the trees, to some steps. At the top go right on a fenced path and follow it along the edges of two fields to reach a horse shelter. Go left to join and go forward on a drive. Cross a stile by a gate and immediately turn right on a path along a fence to walk parallel with a road. At the end, cross a bridge to the road.

Autumn

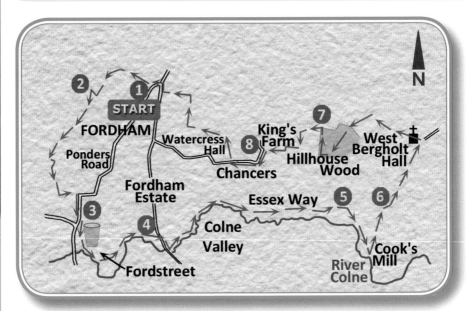

3 Go right and, just before houses on the left, cross another bridge. Do not go through the metal kissing-gate but turn right to walk along the grass with the **Fordham Estate** boundary to the left. Just after the gardens on the right end there is a bridge alongside the **River Colne** (this will deliver you to the **Shoulder of Mutton** if you want refreshment). Our route continues along the bank of the river, now on the **Essex Way**. Soon ignore another metal kissing-gate and turn left (you may, however, follow the river loop and rejoin the route later). Keep forward to regain the river bank to eventually reach a road.

4 Cross through the hedge and go right to walk with the fence on the left (you can carry straight on here if you wish to miss out the rather more adventurous section which follows). Just before a road bridge go left through a kissing-gate. Now you are on access land so you can wander where you wish and, initially, there are no paths. If you follow the course of the river you can cross a stile after some particularly sharp meanders. Now you can follow a very faint path and rejoin the **Essex Way** by climbing a bank. Do not cross the bridge over the river but take a smaller one to go forward. Keep forward at the next boundary with the hedge to the left but, before the end of this field, go left and right to continue with the hedge on the right and go straight across to a gap over a wide concrete bridge. After some brick ruins, go through a gate onto a track. Reach a waymarker.

5 Go right through a metal gate to follow the right field edge. Cross a bridge, continuing alongside the river to reach a junction. We are now going to take a short diversion to look at **Cook's Mill**. Go right through a barrier onto a gravel drive past this wonderful house to a bridge over the river then retrace your steps to the junction. Turn left; this time take the right-hand fork uphill with a derelict house to the left. At the top of the rise, rejoin the **Essex Way**.

6 Go right in front of a pond and fork left before a house to go forward on a track between fields. At the end, fork right to continue with a hedge on the left to reach a small parking area. (Here you have the chance to see the magnificent **West Bergholt Hall**.) Walk down the left-hand side of the churchyard (the church is disused – if it is open it is worth a visit) and exit in the right-hand corner to go left along a track. Soon after emerging from hedges, this track swings left; take a left fork to enter **Hillhouse Wood**. (You could not find a wood that was more packed with

One of the many pill boxes still to be seen along the banks of the River Colne.

bluebells in late April – it also supports blankets of wood anemones, celandine, and wild garlic at different times.) Fork left initially and then keep generally forward, slowly veering to the right to reach a stream at the far end of the wood. Once at the stream, go right to walk alongside it and eventually reach a barrier to the left.

7 Go through the barrier and across a footbridge to walk along the left edge of a field. At the end, follow a waymarker left alongside a mature hedge, which later swings right. Turn left then right below **King's Farm** to reach a lane.

8 Turn left and continue past farm buildings. Go past **Chancers House** and **Watercress Hall**; a few yards after the latter, turn right up steps along the right field edge. Cross a bridge at the end then go left to go through a gate at the far corner. Climb steps to continue on the left edge of a field. Ignore a bridge on the left and go right, still with a hedge to the left. Ignore a track to the left but go left over a bridge at the next junction to continue up the right side of a field and reach **Church Road, Fordham**. Go right and left at the war memorial to go down **Ponders Road** to the car park.

What to look out for –

After the near-panic of the evacuation from Dunkirk at the start of the Second World War there was a very real possibility of a German invasion. All along the coast, defences were hurriedly erected and the Home Guard was formed. In addition to the tank traps and fortifications that lined the Essex Coast a vast building operation started to construct mini-forts called **pill boxes** along the river valleys in case the enemy proceeded inland by boats. Thus, in the relatively short distance that the walk accompanies the Colne we will see four of the structures still remaining as part of what was in fact a prepared battlefield. The examples you see on this walk are octagonal with 36-inch-thick outer walls. They have slits in each side, which are suitable for rifles or light machine guns.

14 Little Braxted

Colemans Reservoir.

The main reason for doing this delightful short walk in the late autumn or early winter is the trees. Quite unusually for Essex, most of the fields we encounter here are lined with trees rather than hedges. Thus, when their leaves are gone we are left with their fragile skeletons, which seem to have been crafted by artistic tree surgeons. The walk passes numerous lakes that are revealed when the leaves fall and the whole route is accompanied by the calls made by the flocks of birds that inhabit the water or the trees. We finish in the hamlet of Little Braxted with its enchanting combination of farm, hall, mill and church.

Distance 2½ miles.

Terrain Much of the walk is on hard surfaces. Although you are likely to encounter some mud at Coleman's Farm, your boots should be fairly clean at the finish. There are no hills and only one stile.

Map OS Explorer 183 Chelmsford & The Rodings.

Starting point The small layby, which will take two or three cars, on the lane into Little Braxted, just before the village sign and a bridge (GR TL833148).

How to get there Little Braxted is on the opposite side of the A12 to Witham. Take the turning off the A12 at junction 22, signed to Little Braxted.

Refreshments There are no refreshments on the walk but you are strongly recommended to continue on the road from your parking place, turning right at the junction, and, in a total distance of 1½ miles, you will reach the Green Man – a pub of some distinction, with a menu that changes daily. ☎ 01621 891659.

The Walk

❶ Start by going forward towards the bridge; just before it, go right over a stile to the left of metal gates. Turn right immediately to walk to the left of a fence and right of a hedge alongside the lane you have just left. Over to the left are the first of several busy fishing lakes you will see on this walk. Turn right for a short way along a drive to the lane.

❷ Cross and follow the drive to **Colemans Farm**. Go left at a fork through a gate to join a farm track, which passes a magnificent barn to the right. Keep to the track, ignoring turnings to the left. Eventually you will glimpse a lake, **Colemans Reservoir**, through the trees. (You can get a better view of the lake and the myriad of birds on it from the occasional fishermen's platforms.) The track becomes a surfaced drive and a gate brings you to a road.

❸ Go right. Take care on the corner; in wintertime you can use the verge but this becomes overgrown. Cross **Appleford Bridge** (notice the weir to the left), joining the pavement on the left for a short distance then crossing right to a concrete waymarker opposite the **Great Braxted** village sign. Go through a metal kissing-gate and keep forward with a fence to the right. At the end of the field, go through a five-bar gate to the right then left to another.

4 Now go forward along a narrow field to exit by a third gate at the far end. Continue forward on a surfaced drive. You will pass between new cattle barns to the left and heavily coppiced trees to the right (the latter hide another fishing lake). When the drive starts to swing right into a farm, leave it to go left on a delightful short path through woodland to reach a lane.

5 Go right, passing the Victorian buildings of **Little Braxted Hall Farm**, to enter the churchyard by a gate. Visit the church (see *What to look out for*). Leave by the main gate to pass **Little Braxted Hall** and then swing right past the mill with its race. Continue across the bridge to your car.

Autumn

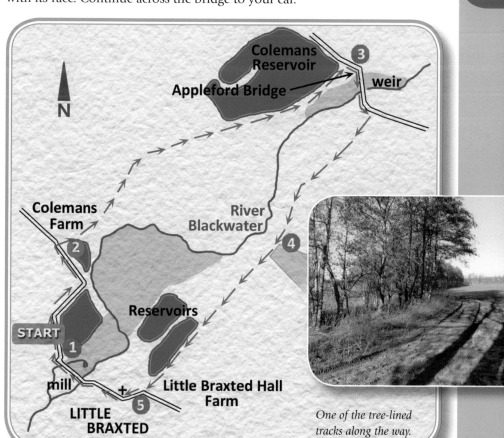

One of the tree-lined tracks along the way.

What to look out for –

The wire gate to the porch of **St Nicholas' church** is designed to stop birds entering the building. Push open the heavy door and be prepared to be amazed. One's first impression is that all the stone surfaces are cloaked in rich tapestry; it is only when your eyes become accustomed to the light that you realise that the effect is entirely the result of paint. The original church dates from the early 12th century when it was thought to be one of the smallest in the county. Over the years there have been several additions and

alterations. The most extensive restoration was carried out in the mid 19th century.

In 1881 Ernest Geldart, an accomplished artist, became rector; it was he who was responsible for all the paintings. 'God's house', Geldart wrote, 'ought to be the finest house, and the most beautiful house in a parish', and that is what he set out to create. His changes were not universally popular because they were accompanied by elaborate services, with vestments, candles, incense, processions and other forms of ritual, which for many people too closely followed Roman Catholic practice. There were letters of complaint in the press and even threats of prosecution but, eventually, there was acceptance. Now visitors come from all over the world to see his work.

15 Layer Breton

The village green and pub at the start of the walk.

This is an excellent example of a big-sky Essex walk that will be particularly good on a windy, clear day in early autumn. 'Layer' derives from 'Legra', which means 'viewpoint', and this gives a clue to the excellent panoramas that can be expected. As with most of our walks, history is never far away and today we start off alongside a moated farm, along field edges and a reservoir to eventually reach Layer Marney with its magnificent clutch of church, tower, house and farm buildings. A return through a rare, for Essex, section of open-access land, with a pub alongside, provides a perfect culmination to the day.

Distance 4¾ miles.

Terrain Easy walking along mainly good field-edge and cross-field paths and quiet lanes. A couple of awkward stiles may be encountered where encroaching hedges have not been trimmed and there may be a little mud after heavy rain.

Map OS Explorer 184 Colchester.

Starting point Park alongside the road that runs parallel to that of the Hare and Hounds – itself a turning to the east at the border between Birch Green and Layer Breton (GR TL944187).

How to get there The starting point is on the border of Birch Green and Layer Breton. It is best reached by a turning off the B1022, which runs between Tiptree and Colchester – this, in turn, is accessed from junctions 23 or 24 of the A12.

Refreshments The Hare and Hounds is open all day and every day. Pleasantly situated at the start of the walk, it provides a good range of beers and food (including a Sunday carvery) in comfortable surroundings. ☎ 01206 330459.

The Walk

1 Return to the main road and cross to a wide gravel path, which leads to a stile alongside a notice to **Breton Barns**. Keep forward with a moat to the left. Just before the end of this path section, go right over a bridge then turn right to follow the field edge to the distant far right-hand corner. At a solid wooden fence with a cross-track go right.

2 Turn left along **Greenfield Houses** to walk along a residential road. At a T-junction, turn left along a gravel path; continuing beyond houses and passing alongside a metal five-bar gate. Keep forward along a cross-field track, which turns left and right but maintains its general direction. Cross the field boundary and another track then climb a reservoir bank to walk with the water to your right before descending to the main path again. Almost immediately go right through a kissing-gate and diagonally left across a field to a gate and bridge combination. Go straight across the next field to reach a lane.

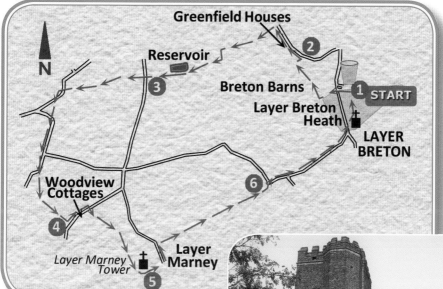

3 Cross to steps and a stile and go forward along the right field edge. At the far end, go right over a bridge and turn left to walk along the edge of a long field. Reach a main road and go left for 50 yards to turn left at a bus stop on an unsigned path, which meanders through scrub to eventually feed into a lane. Turn left and pass a junction. Reach a sharp right-hand bend. Go left over a stile and forward along a fence on the right. In the next field, go diagonally left, aiming for a point to the right of houses and left of a low hedge – here you will find a stile to a lane.

The charming Tudor church at Layer Marney.

4 Go left, passing **Woodview Cottages** and turning right at a fingerpost through a gap in the hedge to go straight across the field to the right of a solitary oak tree. Leave by a bridge and go forward along a grassy path with a deer fence to the right. Ignore side-tracks until you see a metal gate up a bank to the left – this takes you into the churchyard of **Layer Marney parish church.** Go to the right of the church and leave by the main drive.

Autumn

5   Turn left to pass **Layer Marney Tower**. At a junction go left up a lane; as this starts to swing to the left, go right at a concrete fingerpost over an earth bridge and forward on a fine cross-field path. Continue along a line of poplars and cross the boundary, following the field edge to the left to join a lane.

6   Go right and walk gradually uphill past a junction to reach the main road. Turn left. Just past the church go right on a track and soon go left along a wide green pathway. Continue between trees to eventually return to the lane and your parking place.

What to look out for –

Layer Marney Tower, at the start of stage 5, is primarily the creation of Henry, the first Lord Marney, who died in 1523, and his son John, who continued the building work but died just two years later, leaving no male heirs to continue the family line or the construction. What was completed was the main house, the principal gatehouse, which is eight floors high, a fine array of outbuildings and a new church. The Marneys were following the current fashion of one-upmanship; building tall, with lavish use of terracotta and stucco, together with decorative detailing derived from Italy. In building on this scale they were following the example of their monarch, Henry VIII, who believed that a building should reflect the magnificence of its owner.

The tower has had many owners. In 1835 it was sold to Quintin Dick, a successful Far East trader and MP for Maldon. He is reputed to have spent more money bribing his constituents than any other MP of the time. It seems to have worked since he held the seat for seventeen years.

From the top of the gatehouse visitors have magnificent views to the Blackwater Estuary and beyond. On a clear day you can even see St Cedd's chapel on the Dengie peninsular. The tower is open to visitors from April to September; for times see the website www.layermarneytower.co.uk or ☎ 01206 330784.

16 Fishers Green, Lee Valley Park

The impressive King's Weir.

A destination for easy walking year-round, the Lee Valley Park, is especially attractive during the winter for those who wish to avoid the muddy ploughed fields often associated with country walking at this time of the year.

The lower Lee Valley has been extensively excavated for gravel. The subsequent landscaping and management has produced one of the most valuable leisure destinations for East London. Many of the sites associated with the Olympic Games can be found in and around the park.

In the winter there is the opportunity to see the thousands of birds that make use of the extensive lakes and the increased amenities resulting from flooded fields. The walk visits two spacious hides, one of which is a popular spot for seeing the bittern, one of Britain's rarest birds. Besides the birds, a good reason for doing this walk during wintertime is to see the water surging over the two weirs. The return is along the River Lee Navigation. Go back again for marvellous mixtures of trees and shrubs in the summer, followed by excellent blackberrying.

Distance 5½ miles.

Terrain Three-quarters of the walk is on surfaced tracks. In wintertime you are likely to encounter many puddles but surprisingly little mud. Perhaps unexpectedly for a walk in the Lea Valley there is one steep climb.

Map OS Explorer 174 Epping Forest & Lee Valley.

Starting point Fishers Green car park (GR TL377032).

How to get there The car park is to the west off the Crooked Mile, a section of the B194, which runs between Waltham Abbey and Hoddesdon. Turn down by the entrance to Hayes Hill Farm, Stubbins Hall Lane, **not** Fishers Green Lane. If there are no toilets at the car park, you are in the wrong place.

Refreshments There are plenty of pubs and cafés in Waltham Abbey but a little nearer is the Wheatsheaf, which is ¾ mile south of the car park on the B194; it is a McMullen's pub and is open all day. ☎ 01992 711266.

The Walk

❶ Leave the car park at the far end by walking along a path to the left of the toilets. Join a lane and go right to continue past the overflow car park on the left and go through a barrier onto a metalled road with a pylon to the right. You will now have occasional glimpses of **Galley Hill** over to the right. Just before the **Sailing Club** gates go left for a brief detour to **Grand Weir Hide**, from which you will not only be able to see visiting wild fowl but will also get an excellent view of the long **Holyfield Weir**. Retrace your steps to the drive by the Sailing Club.

❷ Cross the drive and turn left into a wide, grassy lane alongside the Sailing Club lake. (This lane has a real countryside feel – wild hedges, tall undergrowth, and the possibility of mud in winter.) At the end, swing right onto an arable field with a hedge on the left and soon begin to climb in the next field. If you occasionally look back you will catch magnificent views across **Holyfield Lake** and the **Lee Valley**. At the top of this second field turn left at a fingerpost to go over a bridge, then turn right uphill to pass a coal duty post and join a drive. Pass a couple of houses and a second duty post and continue downhill. At the end of a fence on your left look for steps going up on the left to a stile.

The River Lee Navigation.

3 Go over the field, with the hedge to your left, cross another stile and continue to a gravel path. Go left, winding your way uphill. Now you have views in all directions – **Lower Nazeing**, **Broxbourne**, **Wormley**. The path settles into a northerly direction then starts twisting and turning prior to descending steeply like an alpine road. At the first loop, leave the path to walk steeply down towards the lake, with the hedge on your left. Go right at the edge of **Clayton Hill Lake**, crossing a surfaced path and then a footbridge at the end and continuing straight across the next field to reach a car park.

4 Turn left along a gravel path, which soon swings right, then left. You come to a lane, which you cross to a grassy track. Now you have rows of greenhouses to your left. Go up steps to a bridge and turn left along **Paynes Lane**.

5 You will walk for nearly ½ mile along the lane and will pass two fishing lakes on the right; at the end of the second, just before a white house, turn right at a concrete tank-trap alongside a telephone pole. Almost immediately go left over a single plank bridge and swing right. Eventually emerge on a wide lorry-track, which you cross, to go forward and then swing right between brambles on a narrow path. Continue alongside railings on the edge of **Holyfield Lake**.

6 Cross the **Kiora Radial Gates** and emerge on a track to turn left in front of a pylon, keeping Holyfield Lake to your left. Reach a bridge across a stream and continue across **King's Weir** – the experience here alone is worth the walk. Once over, go left to join the **River Lee Navigation**. You quickly cross by a bridge and continue walking with the Navigation to your left. Pass the attractive Keeper's Cottage of the **Aqueduct Lock** and keep forward until you are approaching a bridge; here you take a right fork and go left across the bridge.

7 Leave the Navigation and keep forward to the **Old River Lee**. Turn right and just past the **Bittern Hide**, go left over a bridge back to the car park.

What to look out for –

During stage 2 you will pass two **coal duty posts**. These are examples of several different kinds of boundary markers, about 260 in all, which marked out the boundary of London as it was defined in 1861. Most of these posts were erected by the sides of roads and canals and marked the point at which, for a few years, duty became due on coal that crossed the boundary.

17 Great Waltham

The Langleys farm buildings.

Whatever your walking ability, if you are here at snowdrop time you can reach a stunning display of them in a delightful situation within twenty minutes. Having taken in the beautiful setting of the flowers on the banks of the Chelmer with the 18th-century Langleys in the background, many just retrace their steps. However, for those with a bit more determination – and more time – there are other treats in store on this gentle walk. The hamlet of Chatham Green has a pub made out of the remains of a windmill and, after crossing expanses of fields dotted with woodland (and hedges that are bursting with catkins in the spring), you will arrive at the village of Little Waltham, which is rather more attractive than its Great relation. Its quiet streets are lined with richly pargeted houses with the River Chelmer gliding by. Even the new houses have been designed to fit in with the higgledy-piggledy pattern set by their predecessors.

Distance 6 miles.

Terrain An easy walk, usually along wide field edges or farm tracks. Not as muddy as many other walks at this time of year.

Map OS Explorer 183 Chelmsford & The Rodings.

Starting point The Great Waltham village hall free car park, which is signed from the road in front of the church (GR TL695134). This can fill up in the morning but there is street parking nearby.

How to get there Great Waltham is signposted off the B1008, which runs between Chelmsford and the A130. Once in the village, the car park is signposted along with the village hall in the street opposite the church.

Refreshments You pass three pubs during this walk. The Beehive is near the start in Great Waltham. ☎ 01245 360356. Later, at stage 3, you will pass the Windmill Motor Inn where the menu features home-cooked pies with shortcrust pastry, which can be washed down with locally brewed beers. ☎ 01245 361188. Another walker-friendly pub is the Rose and Crown, which is passed during stage 7. ☎ 01245 360359.

The Walk

❶ Leave the car park and turn right. Turn left at the T-junction to follow the road round to the left of the church and pass the **Beehive pub** on the left. At the end of the houses on the right go through a metal kissing-gate and strike out across the parkland. Cross a drive by a pair of gates and go diagonally slightly left to another. Go right on this drive towards **Langleys** (an 18th-century red brick mansion with a commanding view of its park). On a level with the house you will pass the pets' graveyard (see *What to look out for*) and continue between the **North Lodge** and a magnificent group of farm buildings. (It is here, in mid-February, that you will see an enchanting display of snowdrops.) Cross a bridge by a weir and follow the drive to a second bridge, after which you hug the left-hand fence to reach another metal kissing-gate. Now go forward along the left edge of a field to reach a road.

❷ Cross and continue up the left-hand edge of the field to reach the B1008, which you should cross carefully, and, again, continue along the left edge of this and the next field, passing **Chathamhall Spring** wood on the left. You

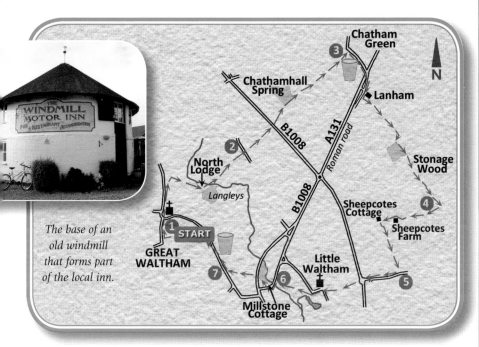

The base of an old windmill that forms part of the local inn.

enter the third field by a plank bridge and continue on the field-edge track to eventually enter a tunnel of trees and emerge on a lane.

3 Turn right through the hamlet of **Chatham Green** and pass the **Windmill pub** with its distinctive round-house accommodation made from the base of the former mill. Reach the A131 and use the crossing island to reach a gap with a surfaced path. Go right at the T-junction and keep forward along what was once the main road. Immediately past a house called **Lanham** turn left at a fingerpost. Once over a stile keep to the left edge of a field to reach a bridge and continue straight across a field where a second bridge takes you along the right-hand side of a hedge, which you follow in the next field to reach a waymarked T-junction. Go right towards **Stonage Wood** and follow its boundary round to the left. At the boundary, go slightly right towards a waymarker on the other side of the field in trees. Go left at the waymarker to walk with the hedge and ditch to your right and continue to follow the right-hand edge of the next field until a waymarker encourages you to strike out straight across the field to a fingerpost on the horizon.

4 Turn right on a wide farm track. Turn right before the gates to a barn of **Sheepcotes Farm**. Cross a stile and follow the track between more barns through the farmyard. Just past **Sheepcotes Cottage** turn left over a bridge. Go

Winter

along the left edge of the field and follow it round for a few yards to go right to the left of a hedge. Cross a bridge on the right and turn left; later cross another bridge and go right to finally reach a road.

⑤ Go right. Cross the roundabout, going between concrete barriers, and continue on another abandoned road. Pass **Little Waltham church** then cross at the corner of the road to follow a fingerpost that takes you diagonally right across a meadow. Go through a gate to join a fenced, surfaced path taking you to a road.

⑥ Turn left to cross the **Chelmer** for the last time. Pass between some wonderful old houses to turn right immediately after **Millstone Cottage** for a short walk along the wooded flood-plain to steps and a road. Cross and go down steps to a bridge and forward to the left of a pill box. After the field boundary, aim for a large house, once a pub, on the horizon and reach a road.

⑦ Go right. Soon after passing the **Rose and Crown** look for a fingerpost on the left, which leads you between a house and a garage to a cross-field path going to the right of a line of garages. Go forward to emerge in a housing estate. Go right then left on the main drive; enter a sports field on the left and continue up its right edge to the road. Turn right to return to the car park.

What to look out for –

Just after passing Langleys during the first stage of the walk, look out for the lines of **small tombstones** to the right. These all mark the graves of the estate families' dogs. Look carefully and you will notice that the majority seem to have been labradors although I like to think that Lassie, who was buried in 1969, was a collie and you will notice that Sonny (1945) was a bulldog. The oldest grave that I could detect was that of Psyche (1902) and the strangest name –Zilla (1939). Pinny's gravestone (1973) bears some poetic lines from Shakespeare:

> *Fear no more the heat o' the sun,*
> *Nor the furious winter's rages;*
> *Thou thy worldly task hast done,*
> *Home art gone, and ta'en thy wages;*
> *Golden lads and girls all must,*
> *As chimney-sweepers, come to dust.*

18 East Tilbury

The reed beds are home to a rich array of bird life.

Whilst East Tilbury may not be amongst the main tourist destinations of Essex, I hope that this route will provide a new insight into the area and a thoroughly enjoyable outing.

At the start and end of the walk we walk through the town, which was designed specifically for his workers by paternalist shoe manufacturer Thomas Bata. The route out to the sea wall is via hedged pathways, accompanied by throngs of birds – in fact a good reason for doing this walk in the winter is to experience the fantastic variety of sea- and land-based birds at this time of the year; it is quite possible to watch oyster catchers and kestrels simultaneously. The stroll alongside the Thames Estuary presents ample opportunity to contemplate the various means by which people have sought to restrain the sea and also harvest its products. These subtle historical references, the remains of groynes and fish traps, are in stark contrast to the Coalhouse Fort, which we reach before turning inland.

Distance 7 miles.

Terrain This is an easy walk over flat countryside. Much of it is on surfaced paths although the return route is across fields and along edges that can be muddy after heavy rain.

Map OS Explorer 163 Gravesend & Rochester.

Starting point Drive through East Tilbury and across the railway to reach a shopping centre with a free car park on the left (GR TQ680785). Alternatively, if you visit during the week and wish to miss out the pavement-walking (where you see the Bata houses) at the start and finish, you could park in streets nearer to the station and start the walk at point 2 (GR TQ678790).

How to get there East Tilbury is signed to the south off the A13.

Refreshments Continue up the road from point 6 and you will find the Ship pub on the left-hand side, a freehouse. ☎ 01375 843041. At the other end of the walk, just north-west of the station along the main road, on the right, is the George and Dragon. ☎ 01375 673177.

The Walk

❶ Walk away from the car park with the post office and pharmacy to your right. Go right at the road to a roundabout. Take the second turning on the left to walk along **King George VI Avenue**. At the end of the road turn left and keep forward to turn right along a short alley. Go through a gate.

❷ Turn right along a wide, fenced, grassy track with a large play area to the left. Go through a kissing-gate to join a surfaced path and continue along a field edge with railings to the right. When the houses end on the right, go through another gate and follow the path to the right. Reach wire gates.

❸ Turn sharp right past a barrier. You are now on a pleasant, well-used and easy to follow path. (This is an area rich in bird-life, attracted no doubt by the extensive reed-beds on both sides of the path.) Ignore a track that goes right in front of wire gates and eventually climb a grassy bank to the top of the sea wall. To your left you can see the storage depots west of **Canvey Island**; ahead you are looking over to Kent.

④ Go right to follow the concrete pathway, which forms part of the sea-wall structure. The concrete path later disappears temporarily but you keep forward over a mound and rejoin it to swing inland and away from the **Thames Estuary**. Now in sight of the **Coalhouse Fort**, keep forward over a path junction. Reach a public footpath sign on the right when very near the fort.

⑤ Go left down a bank to go right over an earth bridge that spans the 'wet ditch'. Just beyond a gun emplacement (minefield control building), go left on a surfaced path. (The fort's location on a narrow part of the estuary means that this is an ideal place to picnic and view the ships going up and down the Thames.) Go right at a T-junction and follow the path round towards a car park and the entrance to the fort (there are toilets here).

⑥ Walk up the road past the **church of St Catherine**. At the brow of the hill go left at a footpath sign. Ahead the landscape is dominated by the power station on **West Tilbury Marshes**. Follow the right edge of a narrow field. Keep forward over a cross-track on a less well-defined path to climb to the right of a concrete

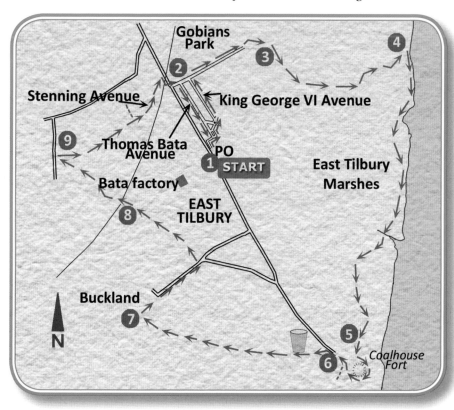

Gun barrels outside the fort.

wall. Descend to continue with the hedge to your right and, for a short time, with a ditch to your left. Now keep forward across the field if the farmer has reinstated the path, otherwise follow the right field edge to reach the far left-hand corner of the field. Cross a ditch to join a pleasant mossy path through scrub. Cross a track with a concrete drive to the left and go right to pick up your path again. Reach the wall of **Buckland**.

7 Go right along the drive past a metal gate to **Station Road**. Keep forward and, just before a fork, go left at a bridleway sign. A hedged path leads onto a cross-field track. (Over to the right you can see the skeleton of the huge **Bata Factory**, which was at the heart of a European 'Bournville-type' town built in the early thirties by the Czech shoe manufacturer Thomas Bata. Besides the characteristic flat-roofed houses, Bata built a ballroom, cinema and many other social amenities for his workers. Unfortunately for the town, changes in fashion and the emergence of cheaper sources of labour overseas meant that most of the operation moved out of the country in the 1980s.) Keep to the right of the hedge ahead, continuing on the left edge of a field to reach the railway, which you cross with care (making sure that you close the gates!).

8 Go forward on a cross-field path to swing right with it alongside the remains of a hedge. Continue under two sets of power lines towards a road. Just before you reach it, turn around at a fingerpost and head back over the field, heading to the right of a line of scrub ahead. Now follow the line of a clearly marked field boundary; when this curves away to the right keep forward to an alley to the right of a house with a conservatory.

9 Emerge on a road and go left then right on **Stenning Avenue**. Later, when this road curves left, go right at a footpath sign along an alley, which takes you to the main road. Go right across the railway then left over the road to the right of **Gobians Park** to follow the fingerpost, turning right into the alley you used before. Go left then take the first right to walk along **Thomas Bata Avenue**. Keep forward across the green to return to your car.

Winter

What to look out for –

Whilst medieval castles hold an almost fairy-tale fascination, there is nothing romantic about the paraphernalia of more modern warfare. The **Coalhouse Fort** replaced earlier, less sophisticated, gun emplacements at the vantage point at this narrow part of the Thames Estuary in the 1860s and with two other forts on the Kent side formed a triangle of fire.

As with many other fortifications along the south-eastern coast it was originally installed as part of defensive preparations, under Palmerston, for the expected invasion from France. It bristled with weapons, which were updated over the years and was only decommissioned after the Second World War. The rather ugly solid structure shows signs of neglect. It is now leased to a project dedicated to its restoration. The website www.coalhousefort.co.uk will give you dates and times for visiting.

Decaying boats litter the shoreline.

This delightful short winter walk features boats, birds and beautiful views. Starting from the bustling Heybridge Basin we set off along the Chelmer & Blackwater Navigation then, after a brief interlude of industrial landscape, we return along the boundary between landscaped lakes and the upper Blackwater Estuary. Here with reed-beds and gorse on one side and salt marsh on the other, the choice of birds to watch and views to record is extravagant. Isolated decaying wrecks of boats only enhance the interest of this highly enjoyable outing.

The Facts

Distance 3¾ miles.

Terrain There are no hills on this walk and many of the paths are semi-surfaced so, for a winter walk, this is relatively mud free.

Map OS Explorer 183 Chelmsford & The Rodings.

Starting point The free Daisy Meadow car park (GR TL871069).

How to get there Heybridge Basin is signposted on the B1026 between Maldon and Goldhanger. Continue about ¾ mile down the road to turn right into the car park just before the end of what is a dead end.

Refreshments Towards the end of the walk you are confronted by two pubs: the Old Ship Inn (☎ 01621 854150) and the Jolly Sailor (☎ 01621 854210). A little further along from the lock is the tearoom called The Lock. This is housed in a tastefully converted former ship's chandlers. The café serves breakfasts, home-made lunches and traditional cream teas from 9 am to 5 pm in the summer with restricted opening out of season (☎ 01621 854684).

The Walk

❶ Walk to the rear of the car park to climb the steps and turn right in front of the boat-hire/snack kiosk. You are immediately walking along the towpath of the **Chelmer & Blackwater Navigation**, which is stuffed with boats at this point. Eventually the boats are left behind and the walk develops into a quiet affair with bushes on both banks sheltering noisy birds and many ducks going about their business interrupted only by the occasional narrowboat. It comes as something of a surprise to be confronted by a new housing estate, **The Lakes**, evolving on the left.

❷ Continue past a footbridge and, after passing a cemetery on the right and attractive new waterside houses on the opposite bank, enter an area of light industry. Go under a road bridge bearing the B1026. (The Chelmer & Blackwater Navigation is about 14 miles long and was built at the end of the 18th century in order to carry goods from Maldon, then an important port, up to Chelmsford. Besides warehouses, some industry dates from this time. Timber was still being transported on the canal in the 1960s.) The towpath later feeds into a lane.

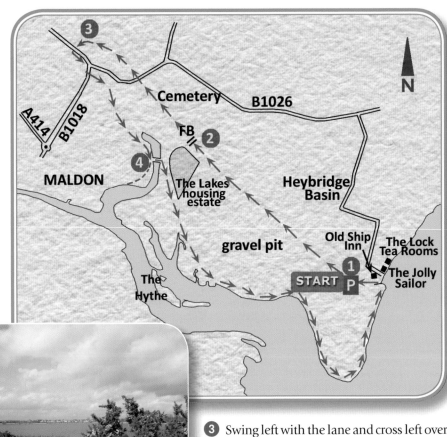

Cemetery
B1026

A414
B1018

FB **2**

N

4

MALDON

The Lakes housing estate

Heybridge Basin

gravel pit

Old Ship Inn

The Lock Tea Rooms

The Hythe

START P

1

The Jolly Sailor

The view over the water to New Maldon.

3 Swing left with the lane and cross left over a rather ornamental bridge and continue to a roundabout. Go to the right, heading for an MOT testing centre. To the left of this, on the ground, is painted a walkway (you may have to hunt for this as cars are often parked on it). This white-lined pathway takes you down some steps into a parking area. Go diagonally right to climb a grassy bank and walk left along its top. This is the sea wall, which you will follow for the rest of the walk. Soon come to a drive, which you cross to continue on the bank on the other side. Now on the other side of the housing development we saw earlier, reach a T-junction with water ahead.

4 Go right for a brief diversion. After a little way the path converges with a fence on the right and it is dangerous to go further. From this vantage point you get a good view of **Maldon** with its suburb, **The Hythe,** to the left. Retrace your steps, crossing the T-junction and continuing towards the houses to swing right with the sea wall in front of them. Once through a boundary you have lakes, the site of old gravel extractions, to the left and the mud flats and salt marshes of the Blackwater Estuary to the right. As you progress you get closer and closer to The Hythe on the other side of the estuary – this at one time was Maldon's main quay and it is still the location of the famous sailing barges (see the *What to look out for* box) and is a fine sight in a low sun with Maldon church rising behind. The lakes at this time of year are teeming with birds – lapwings being especially prolific. All too soon the path returns to Heybridge Basin with its remains of jetties and attractive wrecks of old boats. (Here when the tide is high at weekends there are hundreds of sailing boats competing for the open water.) Go left down steps and cross a bridge over the **Sea Lock** to the **Old Ship pub** to turn left and, once again, walk alongside the canal. On reaching the kiosk turn right down steps to the car park.

What to look out for –

Looking over to The Hythe you cannot fail to see a number of **Thames sailing barges** with their characteristically furled chocolately-red sails or, better still, you may see them sailing in the estuary. A hundred years ago there were over 2,000 barges in the fleet. Many would carry hay and grain around the coast and up the Thames to London

to feed the capital's horses and bring manure on the return trip. These cargoes were known as the 'London Mixture'. The flat-bottomed barges were perfectly adapted to the Thames Estuary, with its shallow waters and narrow rivers. With a crew of only two, which sufficed for most voyages, the vessels were very efficient although by today's standards it would have been hard physical work at times.

The development of the diesel engine in small ships and in large lorries meant that most of the barges' trade was lost. Most of the remaining twenty or so vessels are moored at Hythe Quay where they are available for charter.

(20) Walton-on-the-Naze

The bracing sea wall at Walton.

This is a great walk for fine, clear days and binoculars. Walton-on-the-Naze has, for two centuries, been a seaside holiday resort and this walk doesn't shy away from celebrating some of the remnants of its past grandeur; we return alongside the sea front observing the pier and the sandy beaches.

The main purpose of the walk, however, is the tour of the Naze. This projection (the Old English *naes* means nose) has developed into an interesting wilderness. The dense scrub of hawthorn, gorse and brambles inside the sea wall is a rare habitat for Essex, supporting a rich flora and fauna. It is a breeding place for a variety of birds, including the redshank, warbler and lapwing, and a stopover for migrating birds like the firecrest. Not so obvious but present for the patient observer are foxes, muntjac deer, weasels and water voles. Out in the bay are the mudflats and salt marshes that support waders and many thousands of seasonal visitors. Beyond are views of shipping lanes and the port of Harwich. The northern end of the Naze tends to flood in the wintertime, providing even more habitat for resting birds. So, at this time of year, you gain the bonuses of more birds and far fewer human visitors.

Distance 5¼ miles.

Terrain Choose a fine day for this walk – as soon as you reach the sea wall you will be without cover for several miles. Take extra clothing because, given the exposed nature of the Naze, it can be very windy. These conditions mean that the paths dry out quickly, even after recent heavy rain. This will be a day of easy, level walking with no difficulty in route finding. If you do decide to explore the cliffs and sands, check the tide tables; these are posted outside the café at the start of the walk.

Map OS Explorer 184: Colchester.

Starting point The pay and display car park near the Naze Tower (GR TM265234).

How to get there The most straightforward route is to head for Frinton from the A133 via the B1033 and pick up the signs for Walton. When you reach the sea front, drive north. Keep to the main road, which goes inland then back towards the sea. You will be on Naze Park Road, which leads into Old Hall Lane, at the end of which you turn right towards the tower and car park.

Refreshments As you would expect in a seaside resort, there are plentiful opportunities for eating and drinking. However, many of the establishments have seasonal opening hours. There is a café that is open at weekends at the start of the walk and you will pass several pubs and cafés towards the end of the circuit. You might like to try one of the two venues mentioned in the text. Whites Pie & Mash shop serves traditional 'Fresh Baked Pies, Mash and Jellied Eels'. It is open from Tuesday to Saturday in winter. ☎ 01255 675612. The Queen's Head provides food from Tuesday to Saturday and at lunchtime on Sunday. ☎ 01255 676700.

The Walk

❶ Leave the car park and walk towards the **Naze Tower**, passing the café and toilets on the way. Continue to the right of the beacon, along the line of seats. Go ahead, crossing a concrete track and continuing on a mowed pathway. At a multitude of cross-tracks fork slightly right. Soon fork right again, going to the right of a Second World War block house and continuing downhill. Keep forward at two more forks to swing left along the cliff-top at the bottom. (Even if you don't quite follow these directions, as long as you keep going downhill, you will arrive at the cliff-top.)

2 Pass beside wooden railings to join the surfaced path along the top of the

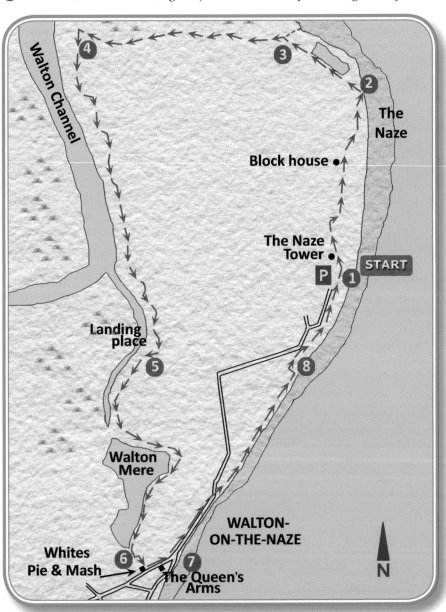

sea wall. Across the bay you now have good views of the cranes of **Harwich**. The surfaced path ends.

3 Continue along an ordinary grass sea-wall path. (You are now between two distinct nature reserves. To your left is the **John Weston Reserve**, run by the Essex Wildlife Trust and named after a prominent local naturalist. To the right is **Hampton Water**, a National Nature Reserve; it is an internationally important breeding ground for little terns and wintering ground for dark-bellied Brent geese, wild fowl and waders.)

4 Eventually you swing left with the **Walton Channel** to your right.

Harwich docks seen across the mudflats.

You have clear views of **Walton-on the-Naze** ahead and the tower, your starting point, to the left. Eventually arrive at a private boat compound.

5 Cross over through a squeeze barrier onto a beautifully manicured path atop another wall, with hundreds of mobile homes to your left (look right to see a couple of concrete boats abandoned on the shore). After the holiday park continue with a school to the left and **Walton Mere** on the right. Begin the approach to the town along the backs of houses. At the end of this stretch there is a waymarker indicating left but you should go right between bollards to continue along a flood-defence wall. Emerge on concrete standing between garages to reach a road.

6 Go left then right. Go left at a junction with **Whites Pie & Mash shop** then left along the **High Street**, passing the **Queen's Head** on the right and some delightful houses on the left. At the end, cross the road to the seafront.

❼ Now, depending on the weather, the tide, and your inclination, you can choose to walk along the shore or the promenade. You can see your destination, the tower, in the distance. Whatever your decision, it is recommended that, in time, you descend to walk alongside the beach huts, which are rather less impressive than those further along the coast at Frinton. Where these huts start to be terraced, climb steps.

❽ Walk across to a surfaced path and go right past a playground. Just before the road go right through a barrier. (Look to your right to see a large off-shore wind farm.) Go left along a very narrow path and emerge to choose an upper path to return you to the car park.

What to look out for –

The **Naze Tower** is a precursor of what became the conventional lighthouse. It was erected by Trinity House in the early 18th century. At nearly 90 feet it was built to support a beacon that aided navigation. It is open to visitors between April and October each year – so plan to return in summer – and houses a gallery, museum and tearooms and, more interestingly, a viewing platform from which, on a clear day, you can see views of Essex, Suffolk and Kent over a radius of 30 miles. The website www.nazetower.co.uk gives details of opening times or ☎ 01255 852519. The Naze, as a headland, has historically fought a battle against the sea, which is eating its way into the cliffs at a rate of about 6 feet a year. Now the tower is under threat; even optimistic estimates say that it will only stand for another 50 years.

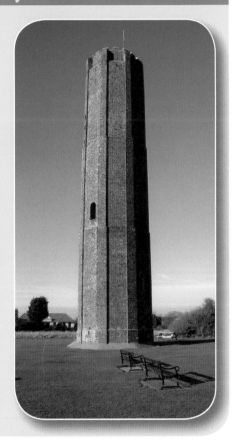